Help Club for Moms

Moms encouraging moms to know the love of Christ

The Wise Woman Grows

The Wise Woman Grows

This book takes you from January – May

Designed by Kristall Willis

Copyright © 2022 Help Club For Moms™

Dearest Friend,

Welcome to *The Wise Woman Grows* Devotional Workbook! We are praying for you to grow deeper in your relationship with Jesus as He reveals His great love to you through His Word and this book!

Why should we be intentional about growing in our relationship with Jesus? The simple answer is when we grow, we become stronger! In Christ, we find refuge from the storms of life (Psalm 46:1). As we allow our Savior to grow us and graft us into Himself, we are less likely to become uprooted in our faith (John 15:4-8). When we stand on the solid rock of Christ, we can be sure that our foundation is firm and trustworthy (Matthew 7:24-27). We can find joy in our trials and unpleasant circumstances, instead of doubt and anxiety (James 1:2-4)!

As mothers, our children see us as a living example of what it means to follow Christ. Being purposeful about growing deeper in our relationship with Jesus is what provides the love, patience, and endurance we need in order to stay faithful to the task that God has placed before us. And best of all, growing is contagious! As we grow closer to Jesus, the flame of our children's desire for Christ will be ignited as well. There are few things in life much more precious or rewarding than that!

Sweet mama, don't be afraid to invite God into all of the "hidden" places of your heart, into the places you would rather not let anyone see. His ways are gentle and kind. He will lovingly show you what you need to change and will cause your life to "bloom" like never before. We are beyond excited for this journey upon which we are about to embark! We pray this will be a sweet season of learning and growing for each of us as we dive into God's Word, allowing it to transform our lives.

Are you ready to begin? Great, so are we! Through this study, we want to challenge you to commit **<u>20 Minutes a Day to a Christ-Centered Home</u>**.

Here's how:

- **Five Minutes of Prayer:** Start your time with the Lord by seeking Him in prayer! Praise Him for who He is and ask Him to reveal ways in which you can grow closer to Him through your time in His Word and your Bible Study. We also encourage you to find a prayer partner to pray with over the phone for ten minutes each week. Praying with another godly woman will change your life!

- **Ten Minutes in God's Word and Your *Wise Woman Grows* study:** Read your study, being sure to refer to all Scriptures mentioned. There are only three studies each week, so feel free to spread each study out over two days, or dig deeper into the Scriptures mentioned on days that you do not have a study. We want spending time with the Lord to be doable for even the busiest mama! Make sure to use the journaling lines to jot down what God has taught you through your time with Him today! Make note of Scriptures or thoughts that stood out to you or write down how you plan to implement the Faith-Filled Ideas mentioned in each study.

- **Five Minutes to Prepare for Your Day:** Before you get up and hit the ground running, take five minutes to plan how you will be intentional about your day. Write down your "Six Most Important List" which is simply six things you desire to accomplish that day. This list can include many things: perhaps a mom tip you would like to do (be sure to refer to the Mom Tips section each week!), a way you hope to encourage your husband or child that day, the meals you plan to prepare, or a task that needs to be finished in your home. Being intentional will make all the difference in both your impact on your family and the wellbeing of your home!

This workbook is designed to help you grow into the woman, wife, and mother you were created to be! As you walk through this study, we pray you will engage yourself in God's Word and open your heart to Him in prayer. Your life will be forever changed by making a habit of spending time with your Savior!

We pray for you to encounter Jesus and grow in spiritual wisdom and understanding as you actively participate in our study—*The Wise Woman Grows*.

Blessings and love,
The Help Club for Moms Team

P.S. – We would LOVE to bless you for buying this book by gifting several exclusive FREE printables to you! Thank you so much for supporting Help Club for Moms; we are so very blessed by you! Check out **myhelpclubformoms.com** to access these printables.

The Wise Woman Grows

What Does it Mean to Grow?

"I am the vine; you are the branches. If you remain in me and I in you, you will bear much fruit; apart from me you can do nothing...If you remain in me and my words remain in you, ask whatever you wish, and it will be done for you. This is to my Father's glory, that you bear much fruit, showing yourselves to be my disciples."

~ John 15:5,7-8

Flourish. Thrive. Bloom. These words describe the Christian life we all desire. As Christ-followers, we have been given the opportunity to live an abundant life; it is our advantage and privilege as believers! The Word says that Jesus came that we may have life and have it abundantly (John 10:10), and don't we all want what Jesus promised?

God as our Creator has given us His Word to be planted inside of our hearts and received with joy. When we hear the Word and understand it, we bear fruit yielding many times over what was sown (Matthew 13:18-23). Too often we think that our imperfections, limitations, and sin keep us from the growth that Christ has for us. But I have good news for you: just like God made and knows every plant on this beautiful earth, He also knows every one of His children (you and me). A good gardener knows what his plants need to flourish, and Jesus is the *perfect* Gardener. He knows exactly what you need to flourish, Mama—the perfect amount of sunshine, pruning, watering, and nutrients that will grow you into the woman, wife, and mother God made you to be.

- Sunshine is the light that shines through you to others as you become more like Jesus by spending time with Him (Matthew 5:16).
- Pruning is the Father tenderly convicting your heart and encouraging you to remove any unhealthy habits or sin in your life (John 15:2).
- Watering is diving into God's Word and seeking what He has to teach you in your season of life (John 4:14).
- Nutrients are new habits and rhythms in your life that honor Jesus and produce thriving, healthy "fruit" (1 Thessalonians 5:16-18).

We pray that through these pages, you will allow Jesus to work on the garden of your soul. Let Him take away the weeds and rubble; give Him the areas of your life that sin has had its grip on for far too long. Let Him tend the soil of your heart, making it His masterpiece. Be ready to experience the blessings that come from our perfect Creator working His wonders and glory in your life!

Love,
Krystle Porter and the Help Club for Moms Team

Plant Yourself Firmly in the Word of God

As we begin to ponder what it means to grow and flourish as a Christ-follower, I can't think of a more beautiful picture than the one in Psalm 1:1-3:

> Blessed is the one who does not walk in step with the wicked or stand in the way that sinners take or sit in the company of mockers, but whose delight is in the law of the Lord, and who meditates on his law day and night. That person is like a tree planted by streams of water, which yields its fruit in season and whose leaf does not wither—whatever they do prospers.

Did you see what the Scripture says will happen to us when we meditate on the Word of God, day and night? It says that we will be like a tree planted by streams of water, which yields fruit and doesn't wither, and that we will also prosper in whatever we do. I don't know about you, but I deeply desire to prosper in all areas of my life, especially in the areas of my marriage and family relationships. We need to understand the love and words of Jesus. He has lots to say about how He wants us to live our lives, but we must plan and make space for the time it takes to spend each day pondering, praying, and listening.

May I invite you to commit yourself to the faithful study of the Word of God through this book? By committing yourself to do each of the Bible studies, you will rapidly find yourself growing into the Christian woman, wife, and mother you were created to be. Since there are only three studies per week, this leaves other days where you can go back through the studies and read the whole chapter where the key verse is found. Remember to record what the Holy Spirit says to you in the journal pages provided. As always, before you begin each study, pray and ask Jesus to speak to you and help you to grow in Him and His love like never before.

Dearest sister, drink deep the words of our Lord, and the love and grace He offers you on a daily basis. When we draw our life from time spent with Jesus and fill ourselves up with His words of love, we find ourselves better equipped to do all that He has called us to do.

Remember, the words of Jesus when He said, "But whoever drinks the water I give him will never thirst. Indeed, the water I give him will become in him a fount of water springing up to eternal life" (John 4:14). When we feed on Jesus, we will never be hungry or thirsty again. Let Jesus fill you as you do this study. His Living Water will help you to flourish and prosper like never before!

We are praying for you!

Love,
Deb Weakly and the Help Club for Moms Team

Table of Contents

Table of Contents

The Wise Woman Grows

Table of Contents

Love Your Husband

Love Your Husband

~ Week One ~

Dear Mama,

A verse keeps popping up in my mind as I reflect on my own journey with my husband. It is found in Isaiah 46:9 (NLT): "Remember the things I have done in the past. For I alone am God! I am God and there is none like me."

This verse is a light of hope for any marriage. God knows the power of remembering. Keeping our relationships' good memories in the forefront of our minds, especially when hard times with our husbands occur, brings tremendous encouragement.

In our marriage, my husband Kim and I frequently utilize this tool to recollect why we are together. How did we meet? What did we love about each other (in the beginning) and why? How did we feel and why did we decide to get married? There are so many reasons to our what, why, and how. Talking and reminiscing about these important events leading up to our "forever" relationship helps keep our love alive!

I don't know what your marriage looks like, whether it's thriving or if you're barely surviving, but God does. As long as you are alive and have breath, there is immense hope for a better relationship with your man. God is God, and there is no one like Him; He can accomplish what no one else can. Put your hope in Him.

I encourage you to take a long walk down memory lane, whether you do it with or without your husband. Take out a journal or notebook and begin to "remember." Write down the pleasant memories, and relive them in your mind. Don't compare them to what things look like in your marriage right now, but allow complete joy to take over! Go back in your mind and bring God into these past experiences; ask Him to rekindle that first love with your husband right now, in the present. Do this frequently, then let God do what He's good at—helping you love your husband *more* than you did in the past.

Love,
Mari Jo Mast and the Help Club for Moms Team

P.S. – Don't forget to print your *free, exclusive printables* available to you at **myhelpclubformoms.com**!

> *Above all, love each other deeply,
> because love covers over a multitude of sins.*
> *~ 1 Peter 4:8*

Mom Tips

By: Leslie Leonard

The **Mom Tips** are designed to help you to grow closer to Jesus,
offer new ideas to help you to grow in your relationships with your husband
and children, and establish a Christ-centered home. At the beginning of each week,
simply pray about which tips to try and check them off as you accomplish them.
Completing them all or doing only one tip is just fine! As we say in the Help Club, *you do you!!*

The Wise Woman Builds Her Spirit

- Set a Scripture as your phone's wallpaper or lockscreen.
- Organize or clean your purse or wallet. It will help you feel more put together.

The Wise Woman Loves Her Husband

Living Room

- Have a breakfast picnic! Enjoy a morning to connect. Get up before the kids to set out the blanket, place settings, and make food. Keep it simple, and have fun with it! If the weather is nice, have it in your backyard. Your husband will appreciate your effort to make his morning special before he heads to work.
- If you want to feel closer to your spouse, do something for others with your spouse. Sounds a little crazy, but it works! Even small acts of kindness performed side-by-side can bring you closer together and help your marriage be more fulfilling.

The Wise Woman Loves Her Children

- Find new perspective. Imagine yourself in your child's shoes: how would you think, feel, and view the world?
- Encourage positive self-talk among your children every day this week. Every time you hear them say "I can't" or "I'm not good enough," stop and tell them that "they can" and "they are good enough." Remind them that they are children of God who are fearfully and wonderfully made. Use Psalm 139:14 to help them.

The Wise Woman Cares For Her Home

- Pick one room in the house this week to deep clean—dust, disinfect, etc. Turn on some worship music and use it as some alone time between you and God.
- Take some time to write down important dates on your calendar or planner.

> " And I pray that you, being rooted and established in love,
> may have power, together with all the Lord's holy people,
> to grasp how wide and long and high and deep is the love of Christ. "
>
> ~ Ephesians 3:17-18

"I can't promise you that marriage will be easy, but I can say that marriage, the way God intended it to be, is a treasure worth fighting for."
~ Darlene Schacht

- A big component of the Help Club for Moms is praying with a prayer partner for 10 minutes once a week. If you don't have a prayer partner, pray and ask God to bring her to you. He is faithful and will provide!

- Good morning my friend! How is your heart? Are you ready to grow deeper in your walk with your Savior today?

- Read Ephesians 3:14-21. The love of God can transform your marriage unlike anything you have ever known!

The Greatest Gift You Can Give to Your Husband & Yourself

By: Tara Davis

Inside each of us is an empty vessel we long to have filled with worth. We seek to receive this value from many places. We turn to relationships, accomplishments, or even a deeply held belief in ourselves to find our identity. Often as wives, however, we hand this empty vessel to our husband and ask him to fill it with our worth. At this point, we become only as good as our husband's performance. When he has a bad day, we are shaken. When he struggles, our value plummets. When he fails to see us through the eyes of Christ, our identity is destroyed. But what if I told you this was never God's plan for you? If you have placed the vessel of your worth anywhere but securely with your loving Savior, you have placed it in the wrong hands.

When we find our identity anywhere but in the Lord, we are left empty, shallow, and always searching for more of what we lack. When we attempt to gain our worth from our husbands, we become selfish, always needing something from them, preoccupied with our longings and how they aren't fulfilling them adequately. We are not able to love like Jesus or to walk in the glorious freedom His love offers!

Sisters, our real identity is in Christ (1 John 3:1a)! He is the only one who can speak over us the truth about who we are and meet our needs according to His glorious riches (Philippians 4:19). When we are finally able to surrender our empty vessels to Christ and allow Him to fill us in a way only the God of the universe is able, we can begin to love our husbands the way the Lord intended (1 John 4:19). Instead of allowing another imperfect human being to determine our worth, we can rest in the unconditional, unending love of the Creator, a love beyond what we could ask or imagine (Ephesians 3:17-21).

When we are filled with the love of Christ, we can pour that love out to our husbands. Only then can we shine the light of Jesus to them in every circumstance and be the friend, lover, and helper the Lord has made us to be. When we are walking in the fullness of Christ, we are able to lay ourselves down and encourage our husbands when they are having a bad day (1 John 3:16). And if they are living outside of God's best for them, our hearts can break *for* them and their struggles instead of *because* of them (Galatians 6:2). This kind of sacrificial love is only possible when our identities are completely secure in Christ. When our needs are met by the Lord, we are free to love our husbands right where they are and pray for them in a powerful way!

In fact, the *very* best gift you can give your husband is to pray that he will know the mighty, transforming, heart-healing love of the Lord! In Ephesians 3:14-19, Paul tells us that the ability to know the deep love of our Savior is only found through the power of the Holy Spirit. Wives, we must pray that our husbands will utilize the power of the Holy Spirit to know the vast height, depth, and width of God's love for them. Loving our husband with a Christ-like love requires us to ask for this knowledge for ourselves as well. Friends, if we and our husbands truly knew this amazing love, our relationships would be transformed! All differences and disagreements would fade in the light of the Spirit of the living God within us. What better gift could you give to the man you married than to pray for him to know this powerful love?

Sister, when you are able to walk this faithful path of total surrender to the Lord within your marriage, a deep, abiding joy awaits you (Colossians 3:12-15)! When you are no longer wrapped up in your marriage and your needs, but are fully occupied by the love of Christ and the act of pouring that love out to your husband, God can begin to heal and refine your marriage through you! Give yourself completely to the Lord today. Pray that you will see yourself through His eyes only and that you will know your identity as His beloved daughter. Dig deeper into His Word to learn about His heart and who you are in Him. Pray, not just *about* your husband, but *for* him. Pray that God would bless your man with this great, abiding knowledge of Christ's love (Philippians 4:6-7). This love will change *everything*, my friend. Believe me.

Questions to Ponder

• Do you struggle with finding your identity in your husband? Would you choose to release him from that today? Would you like to have the freedom to be able to pray for your husband in a heart-changing way? Today is the day to fully surrender to Jesus!

Faith-Filled Ideas

Write Ephesians 3:17-19 on a notecard and place it somewhere you will see it frequently. Pray this Scripture over your husband daily. Pray that your husband will know the love of Christ in his very core, that he will walk in Christ's love, and will live a life that is transformed by the love of Jesus. Pray, also, that you will intimately know this love and that you will find your worth in Him so you can begin to love your husband with the extravagant love of Christ.

journal

_____

_____

_____

Journal

Lord, I pray that my husband would know and experience your abundant love. Let him not grow weary in seeking you and following you. Hold him in your hands and touch his heart in profound ways. Help him to be the man he wants to be. Let him feel your heart for [him], not just for the good he wants to do, not reading your word as only a map or path, but a love from a father, full of wisdom, to a son. Let him feel that this week as I take time to think of him & pray for him. Thank you Lord for Adam. He is my favorite gift you've given me. It makes me cry to think of that. Please bless him and give him all your favor. Deal w/ his heart gently, but allow him to easily follow your promptings. In Jesus name, Amen.

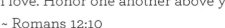

> **Be devoted to one another in love. Honor one another above yourselves.**
>
> ~ Romans 12:10

"Let the wife make the husband glad to come home, and let him make her sorry to see him leave."
~ Martin Luther

- Read Romans 12:10. Meditate on that verse for a minute or two.
- Now, take a few minutes to pray for your husband. Thank God for him. Ask God to show you how to love him better as we enter our devotion time today. Jot down anything that God brings to mind.

Three Tips for a Joy-filled Marriage

By: Krystle Porter

I have been married to my husband for almost 17 years. One of the aspects of marriage I never thought would be an issue is our love for each other. Now, we have never stopped loving each other; however, we have had difficulty knowing what it looks like at times to practically love each other. While most of us may be romantics at heart, I think we quickly realize that isn't always reality! Even still, there are lots of surprises along the way that make the "reality" feel even better than we could have imagined!

Here are three tips I have come up with that have worked wonders in my marriage, and hopefully they will do the same for you. A joy-filled marriage steeped in lots of grace and intentional intimacy, where the best is always assumed in one another is a happy one!

1. Accept your husband's limitations.

> For all have sinned and fall short of the glory of God. (Romans 3:23)

Friends, this is a huge one. Like I mentioned above, your husband will not, and cannot, be perfect, and neither can you. That spot is reserved for Jesus! Your man has his own set of strengths and weaknesses that make him who he is. Over time, I have grown to laugh and even enjoy my husband's imperfections. In a way, it is an honor for someone (especially the one you love most) to show you his weaknesses. His vulnerability is a window into his heart. Don't take that for granted! Pray for him and love him through his struggles, even if these struggles affect your relationship. Before you try to "fix" anything about your husband, go to God in devoted prayer; not just a quick two-minute, disgruntled prayer, but pour your heart out before the Lord. Then wait patiently. Because he knows your husband deeply, you can rest easy that Jesus can do more than you expect or hope. We tell our kids, "Treat others the way you want to be treated," and we heed our own advice in regards to our men. When you inevitably fall short and sin, your heart yearns for grace. Extend that same kind of grace to the one you love most.

2. Be intimate.

> Above all, keep loving one another earnestly, since love covers a multitude of sins. Show hospitality to one another without grumbling. As each has received a gift, use it to serve one another, as good stewards of God's varied grace... (1 Peter 4:8-10 ESV)

I know this topic can scare some away. The fear of being known—*body, soul, and spirit*—is the greatest barrier to the success and enjoyment of your marriage. But God created us for this very purpose; to experience the joy of intimacy like that within the Trinity. Imagine the Father, Son, and Holy Spirit, eternally communing so closely and lovingly that they are always in agreement, yet supporting the Other's distinctiveness. Isn't that what you yearn for with your husband? Start with *intimacy of the soul*. You can experience that through friendship with your man; being interested in his day, asking him how you can help him, anticipating his needs, and being a good listener. *Intimacy of the body*—the giving of our bodies to one another—flows from, and enhances, the emotional connection of soul and spirit. It is God's design for your pleasure and to strengthen your bond. Sexual unity between the two of you is so powerful! Satan would love nothing more than to hinder your marital intimacy through a lack of sex. Friends, remember that God created sex for unity between the two of you. If you find yourself in a season where you are not coming together, pray and ask God to help you! He will! Finally, *intimacy of the spirit* is that deep desire that God created in you to spend time in communion with Him together. This could look like prayer together, reading Scripture together, worshiping at church together, or serving in ministry together. Be creative, but make sure that you are loving Jesus, side by side. Your marriage will be blessed when you do!

3. Always assume the best.

> A fool takes no pleasure in understanding, but only in expressing his opinion. (Proverbs 18:2 ESV)

When you decide to assume the best in your spouse, the whole tone of your relationship will change! It creates trust when you feel like you are on the same team instead of against one another. Conversations become a lot more graceful, and protective walls come down. Assume your husband loves you and cares for you when he is bringing up something that's not fun to talk about. Decide ahead of time that you will work together instead of pleading your individual case in an argument. Bend your ear to understanding instead of winning. When you decide to trust each other with your hearts and not assume the worst in your spouse, conversations that could possibly have turned into arguments become opportunities to grow. It's a beautiful thing!

Questions to Ponder

- Which limitations of your husband's do you have a hard time getting past? List a couple here and decide today to start praying for him and for you to have grace and patience!
- As we thought about all the areas of intimacy, which one stood out to you? What area can you be more intentional about in your marriage? Write it down to work on this week.
- Do you tend to assume the best or assume the worst in your spouse? Write down Proverbs 18:2 (ESV) on an index card and stick it somewhere you will see in your home. Remember to seek understanding and a team mentality when disagreements come your way!

Faith-Filled Ideas

Around our house, we know that when one of us wins an argument, we both lose. So, we focus on making sure that Team Porter (our last name) wins every disagreement. Together we come to a solution that allows us to both "win" and draws us closer because of it. Conflict is normal in marriage, and we are presented so many opportunities to either show love or defensiveness. So, what team are you on? Pray about being on "Team _____" with your man. When a disagreement arises, quietly pray "God help me to be on Team _____, and to not only plead my case."

This simple prayer could be a game-changer for you! Just to note, God may place this on just your heart to do in your marriage. Listen if He does! Jesus changes hearts and your husband can be changed when *you* are being faithful.

journal

_____

_____

_____

_____

_____

_____

_____

_____

_____

_____

_____

_____

_____

_____

_____

_____

_____

_____

_____

_____

_____

_____

_____

_____

> For this is the way the holy women of the past who put their hope in God used to adorn themselves. They submitted themselves to their own husbands, like Sarah, who obeyed Abraham and called him her lord. You are her daughters if you do what is right and do not give way to fear.

~ 1 Peter 3:5-6

"The only known antidote to fear is faith."
~ Woodrow Krol

- It's time to meet with your Jesus! He loves you more than you could ever know and has great things to say to you today. Ask Him to speak to your heart as you read.

- Read 1 Peter 3:1-7. Write verses 5-6 in the journal pages of your workbook.

How to Submit When You're Scared

By: Deb Weakly

Sadly, I have a particular memory etched in my mind that I wish would go away. But before I explain, allow me to give you a bit of the background to the story.

It was right before our daughter's 16th birthday. She had gotten her driver's permit almost a year prior and was about to get her license. She was going places, making lots of new friends, and having fun adventures. Christie was a sweet and godly teenager who was just beginning to spread her wings.

We told her she could begin "dating" after she was 16, and wouldn't you know it, about this time the guys began crawling out of the woodwork to date our sweet, precious daughter.

One of these guys was an 18-year-old guy (man) she had met while performing in an Easter play at our church. This young man was fervently seeking to date our daughter, but both my husband and I had an unsettled feeling about him. As we got to know him better, we both confirmed that he wasn't the type of guy we wanted our daughter hanging out with.

Our daughter was indeed interested in dating the guy, but I was super scared about her spending any time at all with him. My husband felt (much to my chagrin) that this was an opportunity for Christie to learn how to handle grown-up situations like this one and to begin making her own decisions. Normally, I trusted my husband's judgment (he is a very wise and godly man), but this time I was fearful, and honestly, I felt as if I knew better.

So my husband and I began to argue, and argue, and argue. These arguments were the biggest, loudest, most intense ones we have ever had; it was awful. Totally awful. It truly was the most difficult season in our marriage we have ever had, and we have never had a season of arguing like that since.

I wanted my husband to tell the guy to leave our daughter alone, and he wanted her to learn to decide for herself.

During one of our worst fights, I actually cussed at my husband using one of those ugly, no-no words. I was shocked and couldn't believe that phrase came out of my mouth! I grew up cussing like a sailor and some habits die hard, even for strong Christians. I was very disappointed in myself.

But the fact of the matter was, I was scared—really, really scared. And if I was completely honest, I was scared because of my past. I was terrified of my daughter making the same mistakes that I did in my life. This was always my "greatest fear" of motherhood: my children repeating my mistakes. I worried that if she got alone with this guy, he would try to do things that I know she didn't want to do; she was so innocent.

After that day, I was broken. I cried my eyes out to the Lord and asked Him to take control. As always, my sweet Jesus comforted me as I read His Word and sought an answer from Him. I remember reading 1 Peter 3:5-6, and I felt God was telling me to submit to my husband, to do what was right, and to not give way to my fears. I would like to say making the decision to obey and submit to my husband was easy, but it wasn't. I still worried and fretted, and I spent much of my time praying and fasting for our daughter and the situation. After a little while, I was able to feel like I could trust God and my husband with the situation. I moved forward in submission. Even if it was just a little, at least I was moving forward.

My husband and I calmly explained our reservations about this young man to Christie, but told her that we trusted her to make the right decision. We agreed they could meet at a public place so she could get to know him a bit. The entire time she was with him, I was on my knees praying.

I will never forget the day when she came in and told me that she really didn't think they were right for each other. She said that she asked him about his faith, and after questioning him, she told him, "You know, I don't think that you and I believe in the same God." She said that he was very permissive in what he believed was appropriate behavior for Christians, and she wasn't even sure he was a Christian anyway.

My heart was happy and sad all at the same time. I was obviously happy because she had made a wise decision, but I was sad because of the road it took our family to get there. We were all pretty devastated. I fought with my husband because I was afraid. I doubted God's goodness and whether He could truly protect my daughter and keep her heart pure. I wish I would have prayed and trusted God and my husband earlier.

And so here I am telling you my story in hopes that it may encourage you to walk by faith a little more and to trust God to lead your husband and your family. It is not easy to trust our husbands all the time. Sometimes they do make bad decisions, but we still need to trust them as the leaders of our homes, as long as they are not asking us to sin. I have thought often about Sarah, who obeyed Abraham and called him Lord, even when he gave her to Pharaoh (Genesis 12:10-20). God says we are her daughters if we do what is right and do not give way to fear. Fear is a part of life and can be a stronghold if we give in to it. Thankfully, God is with us and will help us to overcome; we just have to trust Him.

Questions to Ponder
• Do you trust God with your life—your finances, kids, marriage, your health?

• Write out your biggest fears in your journal. Be brutally honest and raw. If you don't feel like you can trust God (or your husband), write out the reasons why. Pray and submit these concerns to Jesus and ask Him to help you overcome your fears and unbelief (Mark 9:23-24).

Faith-Filled Ideas
Take a moment to write a "Best Case Scenario" where the situations and problems you wrote about turned out just fine. Think big about God's goodness and ask Him for faith to believe Him to

answer your prayers. Exercise trusting in your spouse and watch what happens. The situations you are worried about may not turn out as you had hoped, but in the meantime, you are obeying God's command to be a submissive wife and learning to walk out your faith in God.

journal

_____

_____

_____

_____

_____

_____

_____

_____

_____

_____

_____

_____

_____

_____

_____

_____

_____

_____

_____

_____

_____

_____

_____

_____

_____

Food for the Soul

There are many ways to show our husbands that we love them. They each feel loved and appreciated differently. Pray this week for God to open your eyes to a specific way to honor your man.

When I want to show appreciation to my husband, I make one of his favorite meals: my homemade lasagna. Periodically, I even surprise him with a date night at home. I feed our kids early and then send them to another room to have a movie night while my husband and I enjoy his special meal together without (too many) interruptions.

Making lasagna is labor-intensive, but definitely worth the work when I see my husband's smiling face. This recipe freezes well, so make extra for later too.

LASAGNA By: Brandi Carson

Ingredients

16-20 ounces ground sweet Italian Sausage

32 ounces ricotta cheese

5 ounces Parmesan cheese, freshly grated

32 ounces mozzarella cheese, shredded

2 eggs

16-ounce box lasagna noodles, cooked as directed

Sauce:

2 28-ounce cans of tomato sauce

4 medium carrots, peeled and finely diced

1 large or 2 small onions, finely diced

3-4 large cloves of garlic, minced

1-2 ounces fresh basil leaves, de-stemmed and finely sliced

Salt and pepper to taste

Olive oil as needed

Tools to make things easier:

- Large piping bag or heavy gallon zipper bag to pipe ricotta cheese on the lasagna

- Small, angled frosting spatula or backside of a spoon to spread ricotta over noodles

Directions:

1. Simmer sauce for a 2-3 hours so the flavors meld together. Preheat a large pot on medium heat and add garlic. Sauté for a few seconds until aromatic.

2. Add carrots and onion. Stir well to combine. At this point, you can turn the heat up a little to medium or medium-high. Sauté until tender and soft, about 15-20 minutes.

3. Add tomato sauce and stir. Turn heat down to medium-low. Add freshly sliced basil and salt and pepper to taste.

4. For chunky sauce, let it simmer for an hour. For smooth sauce, use an immersion blender to puree the sauce. Simmer for at least an hour on medium-low heat. Let cool slightly before assembling the lasagna.

5. While the sauce is simmering, boil water to cook noodles. Add a few generous tablespoons of olive oil and salt to water. Lay cooked noodles out flat, spraying them with cooking oil to keep them from sticking to each other.

6. Preheat oven to 400 degrees.

7. Sauté the Italian sausage and set aside.

8. In a medium bowl, whisk eggs. Add ricotta and season with salt and pepper to taste. Put mixture in a large piping bag or heavy gallon zipper bag to easily pipe onto noodles.

9. In a large bowl, mix mozzarella and Parmesan cheeses together.

10. Spray a 9x13" pan.

11. For assembly, have the noodles, sauce, ricotta mixture, cheese mixture, and cooked Italian sausage ready to assemble in the pan.

    a. Spread a spoonful of sauce in the pan, covering the bottom. Add three rows of lasagna noodles.

    b. Pipe a row of ricotta mixture the length of each lasagna noodle. Use the back of a spoon or a small angled spatula to spread the ricotta out evenly over the noodles.

    c. Sprinkle about 1 cup of the mozzarella and Parmesan mixture over the ricotta.

    d. Sprinkle about ½ cup of the sausage over the cheese.

    e. Spoon sauce over all the ingredients, making sure to cover the noodles completely so they don't dry out. Repeat until your pan is full.

    f. The last layer should consist of noodles topped with a generous amount of sauce and the remaining mozzarella and Parmesan cheese mixture.

12. Cut foil to fit pan, and spray the inside of the foil with oil to keep it from sticking to the cheese before covering the lasagna.

13. Bake for 45 minutes covered, then remove the foil and bake an additional 10-15 minutes uncovered until browned and bubbly.

14. Remove and allow to cool for 15-20 minutes. This will allow the lasagna to firm up before serving.

Love Your Husband

~ Week Two ~

Dear Mom,

I know that at times I need a gentle reminder that I am my husband's companion; not a roommate, not a life partner, not merely a friend or comrade, but his dearest companion.

God made you your husband's companion for this lifetime. You know the little inner workings of your man that no one else gets to see. I believe God gives us a huge advantage in being able to have a looking glass to see into our spouse's heart. We get to see our husband be fully human, knowing that just like us, they have limitations, struggles, strengths, and all the little personality qualities that caused us to love them in the first place! Never forget about the things that drew you to your husband and created the bond you have together!

We can be the apples of our husbands' eyes and heal hurt wounds that have surfaced through the years by having this "companion" mentality!

- Being a *faithful* companion is not always trying to change them but learning how to walk alongside them.
- Being an *uplifting* companion means rooting for them, noticing the good they do and speaking out loud about it.
- Being a *loving* companion means not belittling, but admonishing and encouraging.
- Being a *steadfast* companion means not giving up when it gets tough but having the dedication to stay in the fight with your husband, never leaving his side.
- Being an *intimate* companion means not withholding affection and initiating intimacy.

It's unrealistic to do all of these at once. Ask God to show you this week how you can love your husband well and in what area of companionship you can grow!

With love,
Krystle Porter and the Help Club For Moms Team

Love is patient and kind. Love is not jealous or boastful or proud or rude. It does not demand its own way. It is not irritable, and it keeps no record of being wronged. It does not rejoice about injustice but rejoices whenever the truth wins out. Love never gives up, never loses faith, is always hopeful, and endures through every circumstance.

~ 1 Corinthians 13:4-7

Mom Tips

By: Leslie Leonard

The **Mom Tips** are designed to help you to grow closer to Jesus,
offer new ideas to help you to grow in your relationships with your husband
and children, and establish a Christ-centered home. At the beginning of each week,
simply pray about which tips to try and check them off as you accomplish them.
Completing them all or doing only one tip is just fine! As we say in the Help Club, *you do you!!*

The Wise Woman Builds Her Spirit

• Before you go to bed, write five things for which you are thankful today. Do this three days this week.

• Pray and ask God how your husband and children need to be loved this week. Write down each of their names and the ideas the Lord brings to your mind on a notecard or in a prayer binder. Be sure to follow through.

The Wise Woman Loves Her Husband

• Do you still have your wedding vows? There is something incredibly romantic about the moment you vowed "...till death do us part." Sit across from one another as you say your wedding vows to each other again! Better yet, create new vows that include your children and years together. End with a toast!

• Plan to do a date night kid swap with trustworthy friends. On your date night, your friends will watch your kids, and you return the favor on their date night.

The Wise Woman Loves Her Children

• How do you want your children to remember you? Be that mom this week!

• Take turns playing a quick, simple game with your child in bed before he or she goes to sleep. The card game UNO is easy to play in bed.

The Wise Woman Cares For Her Home

• Get in the habit of making a "6 most important" list before you go to bed. Ask God what He wants you to get done the next day, and write it down. Feel satisfied as you complete and cross off each item.

• Do the "5 o'clock pickup" four days this week. Put on fun music, and set a timer for 15 minutes, as you and your children go through all the main living areas and tidy up. Stop after 15 minutes.

> Be completely humble and gentle; be patient,
> bearing with one another in love.
>
> ~ Ephesians 4:2

"A mentor told me early on, 'Beth, if you treat that man like he already is everything you want him to become, he'll become it.' I could have cut my husband down with my tongue, but I didn't think that was wise. A man needs his woman's love and respect."

~ Beth Moore

- Call your prayer partner for your 10-minute prayer call. If you are having continual difficulty connecting with your prayer partner, pray and ask God for wisdom about what to do. If you feel that she is no longer interested in praying together, call her and ask about it. She may have a good reason for being unable to pray. Always assume the best! If she says that she can't be your prayer partner right now, pray and ask God to bring you someone else. Be on the lookout for this new prayer partner. God will bring her to you!

- It is time to meet with the Lord. He is delighted that you are carving out these moments in your busy day. There is nothing more important!

- Please read Ephesians 4:31-32. Read it again. Pray it out loud and say your husband's name when it says "one another." Hearing his name in the verse will be a powerful reminder of the truth of this Scripture.

Loving Your Husband Even When He is Unlovable

By: Rachel Jones

Showing love to our husbands when we are disappointed in them or they have hurt us is hard. It seems completely impossible. Unlovable behavior deserves harshness and sharp words...at least that is what the world would tell us. However, it is during these times in our marriage that we most need to respond not only in obedience to God, but in a noticeably different way than the world. We need to respond in peace, because a righteous and loving tone is a precursor to the hope our marriages so desperately need.

There have been many, many times in my marriage when my husband has been unlovable; he is human after all. I have had ample opportunity to overlook annoyances, but guess what? I'm human too! From my wicked, self-centered heart, I have made hurtful comments and showed no empathy. It is in these struggles to love my husband that I have learned the most about myself. Looking back, it was often *my* attitude which needed adjustment. This powerful verse has convicted me and helped me to focus on the state of my own heart: "For out of the abundance of the heart his mouth speaks" (Luke 6:45 ESV).

For years, I would not even consider what was going on in my husband's heart that caused him to act in such frustrating or unlovable ways. I only thought of myself and how annoyed I felt, how inconvenienced I was, or how I needed him when he wasn't there for me. You get the point. I realized I had lost a lot of compassion and general goodwill toward my husband. Even though I was let down, I was also letting him down!

Our marriage began to vastly improve when I started living out these verses in Colossians 3:12-14 (ESV):

> Put on then, as God's chosen ones, holy and beloved, compassionate hearts, kindness, humility, meekness, and patience, bearing with one another and, if one has a complaint against another, forgiving each other; as the Lord has forgiven you, so you also must forgive. And above all these put on love, which binds everything together in perfect harmony.

Simply put, I needed to become more tender and compassionate toward my husband by leaning on the Holy Spirit for the strength to do it. Here are three things I have learned about showing unconditional love to my husband:

- **My husband is a good man!**

  And at some level, yours is too. Even if he is not half the man you want him to be, you should still treat him like he is a good man. Look at the quote from Beth Moore today. Treating your husband like the man you desire him to be will cause him to work hard to live up to your expectations! Make sense? Your husband longs to make you happy (even if he rarely shows it), and you need to be his biggest cheerleader. He is your husband and deserves your love.

- **I am often unlovable too!**

  Can we all just make a commitment to accept our humanness and not act like our husbands are the only annoying ones? Apologize to your hubby often and he will likely do the same. Be the first person to start a conversation toward forgiveness. Be more selfless and realize that a happy and healthy marriage can start with *you*!

- **I can do nothing apart from the Holy Spirit!**

  Period. There is little else to say on this matter except: stop trying to improve your husband! Just stop! It is not your job. Your husband belongs to the Lord. You have been given the amazing blessing to respect him, honor him, and love him for your whole life. It is an incredible gift from God to be married, and we need to find hope in the trust we have in Him. Proverbs 3:5-6 says, "Trust in the Lord with all your heart and lean not on your own understanding; in all your ways submit to him, and he will make your paths straight."

Questions to Ponder

- Are you often short with your husband? Do you find yourself frequently losing patience with him?

- When was the last time you looked your husband in the eyes and asked him how he was feeling? Is your husband hard to be around right now because he is going through something difficult?

- I know this might be hard to hear: Is it possible your husband misses his happy and carefree wife, the one who used to delight in him?

Faith-Filled Ideas

Journal for a few minutes about what you love about your husband. Spend some serious quality time praying for your husband and submitting your fears, worries, and frustrations about him to the Lord. Remember, you cannot change your husband; only the Holy Spirit can do that. Your job as a wife is to be an amazing support system who honors and respects your man.

journal

_____

_____

_____

_____

_____

_____

_____

_____

_____

_____

_____

_____

_____

_____

_____

_____

_____

_____

_____

_____

_____

_____

_____

_____

_____

> Her children rise up and call her blessed;
> Her husband also, and he praises her...
> ~ Proverbs 31:28

"It makes a great difference in our feeling towards others if their needs and their joys are on our lips in prayer; also it makes a vast difference in their feelings towards us if they know that we are in the habit of praying for them."
~ Charles H. Bent

- Hey Mama, today you are going to be challenged to love your husband through the power of prayer! So get your Bible, pen, journal, and knees ready! Write the following verses in your journal and commit to memorizing them: 1 Corinthians 10:24, Colossians 3:13-14, Hebrews 3:13, Proverbs 16:32, Proverbs 17:27, and the biggie—1 Corinthians 13:4-8. Challenge your husband to a memory competition!

Loving Your Husband Through Prayer

By: Rae-Ellen Sanders

Marriage isn't easy—lets just put that out there! It is a constant investment of our time and of our emotional support. Thankfully, God in His omniscience knew that we would need Him at the center of our marriages in order to make them successful. I love Ecclesiastes 4:12, "Though one may be overpowered, two can defend themselves. A cord of three strands is not quickly broken." We had this read at our wedding ceremony, proclaiming that we would be strong with Jesus at the center of our union. I've even seen couples braid three cords in front of their loved ones to give Jesus this authority.

When we enter into a covenant relationship with God and our spouse, we are agreeing to the great responsibility of being our husband's helpmate, till death do us part. But if you haven't realized yet, we can't do it without God's help. Prayer provides the overcoming power to endure the hardships of marriage! It removes uncertainty and provides peace and confidence. God doesn't care how eloquent our words are; He simply wants us to seek Him! This open communication that we have with God the Father does not come with hoops to jump through or conditions. When we come before the throne of grace with our concerns, our gentle and loving Abba daddy hears us. Prayer invites the Holy Spirit to work in us and through us to shine His love.

No one else knows our men as well as we do. We hold the unique privilege and power to intercede for them through prayer! What does intercede mean? It means to intervene on behalf of another. All of us have obstacles in our marriages that need heavenly intervention. God can give us answers when we seek Him. Ask the Lord for understanding and patience, and for discernment of your husband's needs. Ask for humility for you and your husband, and the grace to trust that God is at work. Jesus resists the proud, so drop the act and plead for God to intervene in your marriage.

News update: Throughout time, there has not been one perfect marriage. It started with Eve, who gave her husband bad advice, and now we all reap the tragic consequences in our own relationships. Thankfully, our gracious Lord offers to help us navigate through our differences and perspectives, drawing us together in unity.

Guided prayers are amazing! I love to look back over them and get new inspiration. Praying written prayers also keeps me on track to cover my husband from head to toe. I have listed several books on praying for your spouse at the bottom of this study. Comb through these to find the right one for you.

Commit to praying for your husband and your marriage daily. Watch God move in you and your spouse in a fresh new way! Make your appeal to the Lord and trust that God wants the very best for your marriage. Pray for every area of his life: his faith and spiritual walk with God, his emotions, communication, finances, freedom from lust, knowing purpose, loving deeply, physical protection, pursuing gentleness, raising children, role as leader, security at work... just to name a few.

Here are a few lines I personally pray that you are welcome to use too:

> *Father God, continue to transform my husband into Your image. Strengthen him in his weakness, give him wisdom at work, and help him to overcome difficulties with the help of the Holy Spirit. Guide his thoughts and words. Create in him a hunger and thirst for You so he will seek You above all things. Enable my husband and me to love one another deeply as a reflection of Your love. Give me a grateful heart for my husband's efforts on my behalf, and teach me to affirm and appreciate him. Bless our marriage and our home life. May You be our anchor, in Jesus' name. Amen.*

Questions to Ponder

• Do you pray for your husband daily? Do you thank the Lord for the precious gift of your husband? If you are honest, do you use words to build him up (1 Thessalonians 5:11)? There is no better time than right now to make a prayer list of things in your marriage that need the Lord's covering and blessing. Then be purposeful and PRAY!

Faith-Filled Ideas

Intentionally create moments free of distraction to pray together. Ask your husband to read Scripture together (Ephesians 5:25-27). Show love to your husband in his love language; do the things that he needs to fill his bucket. Make sure to appreciate the effort given on his part even if it seems miniscule. Affirm him with words of appreciation and approval. Whether your marriage is a strong, three-stranded cord or hanging by a thread, prayer will make a positive difference! You can do this! According to Proverbs 31:28-29, wives flourish in this role!

Guided Prayers for Your Husband:

Prayer of Blessing Over Your Husband by Bruce Wilkinson

Power of a Praying Wife by Stormie Omartian

Power of Prayer to Change Your Marriage by Stormie Omartian

Praying for Husband from Head to Toe by Sharon Jaynes

31 Days of Prayer for My Husband by Jennifer Smith

31 Prayers for My Future Husband by Jennifer and Aaron Smith

Praying God's Word for My Husband by Kathi Lipp

Praying God's Will for My Husband by Lee Roberts

Praying Like Crazy for Your Husband by Tamyra Horst

7 Guided Prayers for Your Husband by Bruce Wilkinson and Heather Hair

Journal

_____

_____

_____

_____

_____

_____

_____

_____

_____

_____

_____

_____

_____

_____

_____

_____

_____

_____

_____

_____

_____

_____

_____

_____

_____

> *Kind words are like honey—sweet to the soul and healthy for the body.*
> ~ Proverbs 16:24 (NLT)

"Kind words do not cost much. Yet they accomplish much."
~ Blaise Pascal

- Good morning Mom! Our study today teaches us about the huge impact our words have in our marriages. What we say, and more importantly, how we say it affects the course of our relationships, for better or worse. When we are intentional about choosing kind and loving words, we reap incredible blessings in our marriages!

- Read Proverbs 18:4 and Proverbs 18:20.

Our Words: An Invitation to Peace or the Provoking of War

By: Mari Jo Mast

We've all heard the saying, "Sticks and stones will break my bones, but words will never hurt me." I cannot think of a more untrue quote. On the contrary, our words are ultra powerful. Hurtful words can be so potent. They have the power to bring extreme mental anguish and painful damage to the heart of the one receiving them. What we say can provoke a continual emotional war in the mind.

However, life-giving words are even more powerful. They bring tremendous life, healing, strength, and peace. As you read today in Proverbs 18:4 (NLT), Solomon wrote, "A person's words can be life-giving water; words of true wisdom are as refreshing as a bubbling brook."

What a beautiful word picture. I know most of us have experienced it firsthand—a timely word spoken or encouragement by a friend in a dry season. It can be so life-altering and helps to shovel you out of a deep pit, and set you on the right path again.

When communicating with our husbands, it's so important to select words wisely. Words are free, and can be put together in many ways. If we choose to speak from the flesh, our words become quite costly, damaging relationships, especially over time with our husbands. As Proverbs 18:21 (GNT) warns, "What you say can preserve life or destroy it; so you must accept the consequences of your words."

The way we become better at inviting peace with our words is to pay attention to what we're thinking about or meditating on. *We will not speak out what we haven't thought about.* (Take a moment to think about this).

When we have trouble clearing our head of unforgiving thoughts, we should go back to the cross and ask Jesus to help us. Remember what we've been forgiven from. God isn't keeping a record of our wrongs. He genuinely loves and forgives us, even though we've sinned against Him a thousand times. God's thoughts toward us are continually good (Jeremiah 29:11, Psalm 139:16-18, Isaiah 55:8-9,

Psalm 40:5). Meditating on His undeserved grace brings thoughts of peace and love which will pour out onto our spouses.

Difficult seasons in our marriage (for whatever reason), can either make us stronger and superior or turn us sour and resentful. With the power of the Holy Spirit, we are able to forgive and think on good things. These healing thoughts become life-giving words of love and kindness to our husbands!

Philippians 4:8 (NLT) says:

> And now, dear brothers and sisters, one final thing. Fix your thoughts on what is true, and honorable, and right and pure, and lovely, and admirable. Think about things that are excellent and worthy of praise.

The key word in this Scripture is *fix*. According to the Merriam-Webster dictionary, it means: to hold or direct steadily, to capture the attention of, to set or place definitely, or to make an accurate determination. We need to focus (fix our thoughts) on good things, not evil.

1 Peter 4:8 (NLT) says:

> Most important of all, continue to show deep love for each other, for love covers a multitude of sins.

Wow! It doesn't say a few sins; it says a *multitude* of sins. I think Peter understood that all of us are guilty of committing innumerable sins in our lifetimes! No one is exempt.

Sweet mom, don't keep a mental list of the sins of your husband. Instead, overlook them and show him the deep love of God. When you remember the blood of Jesus that wiped away all of your sin (past, present, and future), it becomes so much easier to let go of offenses. God's not keeping track and neither should you! A miracle of restoration can begin in your marriage when you focus on everything your spouse does right, rather than on his mistakes.

God wants you to thrive in your marriage, not just survive! Thriving begins when you choose to listen to the Holy Spirit's thoughts, and cast down your fleshly ones. When you receive His life-giving, higher thoughts, their fruit will be words of healing, life, and peace!

Let's think before we talk. Let's invite peace into our marriages, instead of provoking war.

Questions to Ponder

- How are you using your words in your marriage? War or Peace?

- When your words or tone are harsh or unkind, go back and pinpoint why. What were you believing? What were you feeling? Journal your answers.

- Think about any unforgiving thoughts you've had and their effect. How has resentment impacted you and your relationships?

Faith-Filled Ideas

Bring your accusations to Jesus and hand them over completely to Him. Do the right thing; choose to forgive. Thank Jesus you are forgiven for your own sin and ask the Holy Spirit to fill you in any place you hurt. Praise Him for giving you grace instead of the justice you deserve. Last of all, give God your mouth. Ask Him to help you build up your husband, not tear him down.

journal

_____

_____

_____

_____

_____

_____

_____

_____

_____

_____

_____

_____

_____

_____

_____

_____

_____

_____

_____

_____

_____

_____

_____

_____

_____

_____

_____

Journal

_____
_____
_____
_____
_____
_____
_____
_____
_____
_____
_____
_____
_____
_____
_____
_____
_____
_____
_____
_____
_____
_____
_____
_____
_____
_____

Prepare for the Unexpected

By: Kelly Smith

*"Trust in the Lord with all your heart and
lean not on your own understanding;
in all your ways submit to him, and he will make your paths straight."*

~ Proverbs 3:5-6

On April 20, 2016, my husband Doug unexpectedly went home to be with Jesus. Through our pain and the great sense of loss, God has graciously given my four children and me the strength to endure and continue to fight the good fight in spite of heartbreak. Adjusting to life without the man we all loved and depended upon has taught me many life lessons about handling those unwanted events and circumstances that can happen to us all out of the blue. Here are some things I want you to know to be prepared for hard times...

First and foremost, it's important to have a good church home. Hebrews 10:24-25 tells us to "consider how we may spur one another on toward love and good deeds, not giving up meeting together, as some are in the habit of doing, but encouraging one another—and all the more as you see the Day approaching." If my family did not have a body of believers who came alongside to comfort, help, and minister to us through this sad time, it would have been so much more difficult to move forward. Many people were there for us in the first few months, but as time moved on, understandably, so did many of these people. However, the body of believers in our church home continue to help when I need a handyman, car maintenance, financial guidance, childcare, etc.

Secondly, be informed about the business of managing and protecting your household. Here is a partial list of things to consider now. Create a file or binder with this information so you or your loved one can access these important documents at a moment's notice. *Note:* This checklist is for informational purposes only and not for providing legal advice. Please consult an attorney for more specific information for your family.

- Have wills, medical directives, and Power of Attorney for both spouses. Put in writing what medical decisions each of you would want the other to make on your behalf. Consider what happens if you and your husband both die: who will care for your kids if you both pass?

- Know your spouse's funeral and burial wishes. If possible, buy plots and headstones ahead of time.

- Hold all property and accounts jointly, with both names on the ownership documents. Double check with your bank that you are both listed as account owners with the same privileges in case something happens to one of you.

- Know names and contact information for your accountant, financial advisor/manager, lawyer, and insurance agent(s).

- Have a complete list of assets and their values.

Prepare for the Unexpected

By: Kelly Smith

- Be the designated beneficiary on custodial/IRA accounts or accounts/holdings solely owned by your spouse.

- Have at least one credit card in your name.

- Request at least 8 death certificates from the funeral home or whoever provides it. (Getting copies later is difficult and time-consuming).

- Keep all vital information in one secure, fire-safe location. This includes:

  - List of all accounts, logins, passwords, and URL's, as well as email accounts
  - Life insurance policies
  - House and vehicle insurance policies
  - Official copies of wills, medical directives, and Power of Attorney
  - Vehicle titles
  - Mortgage and loan documents
  - Deeds
  - Banking and investment statements and account numbers

  - Social Security statement
  - Safety deposit box key and location
  - Keys and combinations for all locks
  - Social Security cards and birth certificates for everyone in the household
  - Marriage license
  - Military discharge papers and veteran's benefit statement
  - Business account information and access
  - Directives for business

** If you or your spouse own a business, familiarize one another with your roles, and maintain relationships with all financial and operations managers.

Finally, always remember that through Christ, you will overcome. As a little girl, Corrie Ten Boom experienced the death of a neighbor. Corrie began to worry about her parents dying. One day, while speaking with her daddy, Corrie told him of her concern.

> [Corrie] burst into tears, "I need you!" [she] sobbed. "You can't die! You can't!" "Corrie," he began gently. "When you and I go to Amsterdam, when do I give you your ticket?" "Why, just before we get on the train." "Exactly. And our wise Father in heaven knows when we're going to need things, too. Don't run out ahead of him, Corrie. When the time comes that some of us will have to die, you will look into your heart and find the strength you need – just in time." (*The Hiding Place*)

God will give us everything we need right when we need it. Trust Him for that promise!

Prepare for the Unexpected

By: Kelly Smith

SCRIPTURES TO REFERENCE:

*"Be strong and courageous.
Do not be afraid or terrified because of them,
for the Lord your God goes with you; he will never leave you nor forsake you."*

~ Deuteronomy 31:6

"I will refresh the weary and satisfy the faint."

~ Jeremiah 31:25

*"He gives strength to the weary
and increases the power of the weak.
Even youths grow tired and weary,
and young men stumble and fall;
but those who hope in the Lord
will renew their strength.
They will soar on wings like eagles;
they will run and not grow weary,
they will walk and not be faint."*

~ Isaiah 40:29-31

*"Trust in the Lord with all your heart and
lean not on your own understanding;
in all your ways submit to him,
and he will make your paths straight."*

~ Proverbs 3:5-6

*"Come to me, all you who are weary and burdened, and I will give you rest.
Take my yoke upon you and learn from me, for I am gentle and humble in heart,
and you will find rest for your souls."*

~ Matthew 11:28-29

How does Jesus say we should LOVE?

FOR KIDS!

TEACH YOUR KIDS ABOUT HOW GOD WANTS US TO LOVE EACH OTHER!

God is so good to us to give us a blueprint of LOVE to follow as we seek to love our family and those in our circle well.
1 Corinthians 13:4-7 maps it out for us perfectly.

FOR THIS ACTIVITY:

1. Cut out the large heart and small hearts on the next page.

2. As you read 1 Corinthians 13:4-7, tell the kids to find the small hearts with the words they hear in the verses and place them in the large heart.
(Feel free to glue them on as well for a decoration for your home!)

3. Talk to the kids about each phrase in the small hearts. Explain that this is how God wants us to love others.

4. Pray to end your time and ask God to help each of you love in the way His Scripture tells us!

*** Color Printable found at myhelpclubformoms.com ***

How does Jesus say we should LOVE?

FOR KIDS!

PATIENT

KIND

DOES NOT ENVY

IS NOT PROUD

DOES NOT BOAST

NEVER DISHONORS OTHERS

NOT SELF SEEKING

NOT EASILY ANGERED

KEEPS NO RECORD OF WRONGS

REJOICES IN TRUTH

LOVE IS...

1 Corinthians 13:4-7

ALWAYS PROTECTS

ALWAYS TRUSTS

ALWAYS HOPES

ALWAYS PERSERVERES

*** Color Printable found at myhelpclubformoms.com ***

Spiritual Parenting

We all know It's hard enough to train kids to behave, but good behavior isn't what Jesus calls for in the Bible. He wants hearts and souls that are shaped in vibrant faith and love toward God and others. How can parents cultivate this in their children?

For the next two weeks, Dr. Michelle Anthony shares practical examples and biblical insight on the spiritual role of parenting. We know you will be blessed!

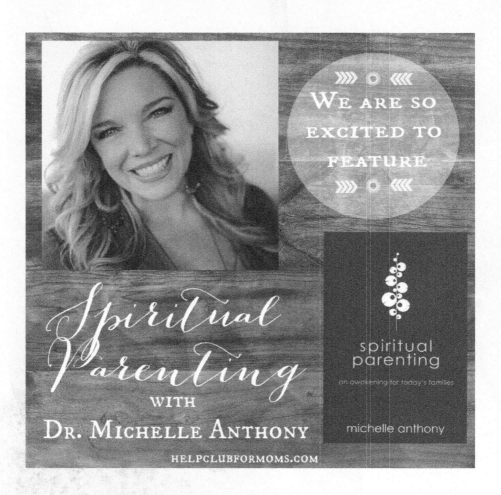

WE ARE SO EXCITED TO FEATURE

Spiritual Parenting
WITH
DR. MICHELLE ANTHONY
HELPCLUBFORMOMS.COM

spiritual parenting
an awakening for today's families
michelle anthony

Spiritual Parenting

~ Week Three ~

Dearest Mom,

Parenting is hard. Parenting in our own strength is even harder. So why do we have the temptation to do this monumental thing apart from our Savior? It's because we, myself included, often lose sight of His hand over our lives. Please read John 15:1-10 for a beautiful illustration of this from the Word of God.

For the next few weeks, I would like to challenge you to simply grow in Jesus. Small growth is fine: five more minutes in your Bible a day or an extra prayer quietly to yourself before you get out of bed in the morning. Any type of growth and flow toward Him is good. These small habits will become routine, I promise. He calls us to be connected to Him at all times. He yearns for our lives to be a constant outpouring of Him and His faithfulness.

As parents, we are more fruitful when we are connected to the root system of God. As we grow in Him, He prunes and guides us in parenting. I was telling my husband recently how I am tempted to think that I am doing such a great job as a mom and that I have no troubles. I sometimes think, "Oh, this mothering thing is not too hard." But you know what is funny? Everything "good" I do as a mother is from the Lord! John 15:5 (ESV) says, "I am the vine; you are the branches. Whoever abides in me and I in him, he it is that bears much fruit, for apart from me you can do nothing." Throughout the last decade, God has constantly been speaking to me and refining me; He deserves the glory when I parent well. I want to remember that, and I encourage you to remember it as well.

If we remain in Him, we can ask for help and He will gladly come alongside us (John 15:7). However, if we push Him aside and try to parent in our own strength, it won't go well. We are all ambassadors of Christ's love to our children. God has blessed us immensely with these precious children, and it is our duty to communicate His love and tenderness toward them. I am praying for you this week, friend.

Blessings and love,
Rachel Jones and the Help Club for Moms Team

> " *This is the vision for us as spiritual parents:*
> *We persevere in loving Christ in our hearts and by our actions, in trusting*
> *in Him for what only He can give, and then modeling this to our children.* "
> *~ Dr. Michelle Anthony*

Mom Tips

By: Leslie Leonard

"Let your roots grow down into him, and let your lives be built on him.
Then your faith will grow strong in the truth you were taught,
and you will overflow with thankfulness."

~ Colossians 2:7 (NLT)

The Wise Woman Builds Her Spirit

- Ask a mom and her kids on a play date.

- Write Romans 12:2 on your chalkboard, mirror or a notecard to keep at your kitchen sink. Commit to memorizing the verse by the end of the week. For further study and growth, read Romans 1:18-3:20 and journal about how you/we can cultivate a renewed mind.

The Wise Woman Loves Her Husband

- Write 1 Corinthians 16:13 on a notecard, and slip it into your husband's work bag. Pray for your husband to have courage in all that he does, in and out of the home.

- Take time this week to pray with your husband. Ask God how He wants to shape you as parents and how to set the tone of your home.

The Wise Woman Loves Her Children

- Every day this week, ask your kids something new. Instead of "How was your day?" or "How was school?," ask something like "How can I pray for you tonight?" "What was the best part of your day?" What did you do to have fun today?" or "What did you do to grow closer to God?"

- Offer a blessing over your children this week. Look them in the eyes, touch them with your hands, tell them you love them, and pour into them all your heart desires to say. Do not worry about what to say; the Holy Spirit will guide you.

The Wise Woman Cares For Her Home

- Double your recipe for dinner one night. Box up leftovers for tomorrow, or take a meal to a single or elderly neighbor.

- It's time for spring cleaning! Get printable spring cleaning check lists from Pinterest to kickstart your housework.

So here's what I want you to do, God helping you:
Take your everyday, ordinary life—your sleeping, eating, going-to-work,
and walking-around life—and place it before God as an offering.
Embracing what God does for you is the best thing you can do for him.

Don't become so well adjusted to your culture that you fit into it without even thinking.
Instead, fix your attention on God. You'll be changed from the inside out.
Readily recognize what he wants from you, and quickly respond to it.
Unlike the culture around you, always dragging you down to its level of immaturity,
God brings the best out of you, develops well-formed maturity in you.

~ Romans 12:1-2 (MSG)

"At the heart of our Christian faith is a story...Unless the story is known, understood, owned, and lived, we and our children will not have Christian faith"
~ John H. Westerhoff

- A big component of the Help Club for Moms is praying with a prayer partner for 10 minutes once a week. If you don't have a prayer partner, pray and ask God to bring her to you!! He is faithful and will provide!

- Open your Bible to Hebrews 11 and read what is called the "Hall of Faith" in Scripture. What do you notice in each of the people mentioned in this history of our faith?

Creating an Environment of Storytelling

By: Dr. Michelle Anthony

While today's culture is telling our children that life is "all about me," we can direct them to think about the fact that life is really "all about God."

God's Word is basically a love story—a story of the Divine Lover pursuing His created ones in order to have a personal relationship with each one of them. In His story, He is the main character. Sometimes I am tempted to believe that I am the main character, that the story is really about me—because after all, I am in every scene. But that's a lie. It's a lie that our children are told on every TV channel, in every advertisement, and in every song.

Can you see how dangerous Satan's lie is? If he can get me to believe that this life is a story centered around me and my happiness, then I will see life as a series of events that allow me either to succeed or fail in this endeavor. I begin to subtly make decisions that will be to my own benefit. After all, don't we always want the main character of a novel to be victorious in the end? We want her to succeed and be happy. The problem with this perspective is that life is hard and unfair sometimes. I can't always control life, events, and other people. Then what? If we consistently tell our children the Big God Story, who God is and how He has chosen a part for each of us to play, we then realize that we can never play the role of the main character. When this happens, we are able to worship God and not ourselves. We are free to be who we were created to be: true worshippers in every aspect of our lives!

With this in mind, let's consider sharing the Bible's content in the context of its original story line. Often we tell fragmented stories of God, Jesus, or other characters in the Bible, and we do so in ways that aren't linear. Even most children who know the stories of the Bible can't tell you whether Abraham was born before David, or if baby Jesus was alive when baby Moses was. We teach Bible stories in isolation and often don't tell the bigger story where God is central. Instead, baby Moses is the key figure one day, then Noah the next, and Jesus is merely one among many in this ancient storybook of interesting people.

However, by putting each story in the context of the main story—God's story, we elevate Jesus, the Redeemer, to His rightful place in the story line. In the Big God Story, Jesus is the hero. We can tell our children the narrative of history in the context of the big picture, and create opportunities for them to put what they are learning into action.

Take a moment and think about your story. Think about your beginnings and your family of origin. How did God use the circumstances in your life—both the positive and the negative—to bring you to Himself? At what point or points in your life did you recognize God's intervention? We are all sinners, and we all need a Savior. We all have been redeemed, and we all have a story. Of course God has a different journey for all of us, but as we live and share our faith experience, it gives our children the hope of something more, something bigger than the perceived enormity of their present situation.

Romans 12:1-2 reminds us that God is calling us out of the "way" that the world sees and does things and wants to reorient our lives into the "script" He has written for us. It is essential that we find our part to play in His story. From there, we can help our children to catch a glimpse of the storyline that they are a part of and to step into the role for which they have been uniquely prepared and gifted.

Questions to Ponder

- When was the last time you told your "story"? Have you ever shared this with your children? What fears might you have in sharing it?

- In what ways have you made "other characters" of the Bible more central than God Himself? How can you start today to make God the main point?

- What roles do you perceive that God might have for your child in His great narrative? What unique qualities has He possessed him/her with that will build His kingdom?

Faith-Filled Ideas

Here are some ideas to help make storytelling alive in your home:

1. Learn the Big God Story yourself. Purchase a chronological Bible and/or *The Big God Story* children's book that I wrote and start working your way through the grand redemptive narrative.

2. After reading any passage in the Bible or picking your child up from church, ask this question: "What do I know about God?" As you do this, you will come up with a God statement such as "God is Powerful," or "Jesus is Compassionate." Ultimately, this will shape you more than learning about what a certain character did or did not do in the Bible.

3. Practice sharing your "story." It is powerful and will encourage your children to see how God has used both the good and bad in your life to accomplish His redemptive work!

journal

> " And you also were included in Christ when you heard the word of truth, the gospel of your salvation. Having believed, you were marked in him with a seal, the promised Holy Spirit, who is a deposit guaranteeing our inheritance... "
>
> ~ Ephesians 1:13-14a (NIV, 1984)

"The Bible does not begin with the Fall but with Creation. Our value and dignity are rooted in the fact that we are created in the image of God, with the high calling of being His representatives on earth. In fact, it is only because humans have such high value that sin is so tragic...[But] He restores us to the high dignity originally endowed at Creation—recovering our true identity and renewing the image of God in us."

~ Nancy Pearcey

- You are a daughter of the most-high King. The Lord Jesus has given you a place in His family because of His great love for you. In this moment, choose to accept this extraordinary gift of belonging and identity.

- Open your Bible and read about our identity in Christ in Ephesians 1:3-14.

- Take time to soak in each abundant and extravagant word that is being spoken about you in Christ.

Creating an Environment of Identity

By: Dr. Michelle Anthony

When we start to realize how amazing God's story is, a question naturally arises: "Who am I that I should get to be a part of the greatest story ever told?" Think about that question. How would you answer it? Is there a set of right answers that comes to your mind? Or do you struggle with knowing what that really means? Do you have a sense that God, the Creator of all things, created you for a unique purpose? The fact that you and I are even invited to be a part of God's grand narrative of life, love, and redemption is true only because of Christ. This is why we affirm that our identity with God is found in Christ.

When I became a mother, I desperately wanted my children to recognize their unique God-given identity. God began to reveal to me why my identity was foundational for the kind of faith that I wanted them to possess. For the first time, I was awakened to the reality of who I believe God created me to be and what plan I believe He had for me to fulfill.

This awakening began to shape the way I viewed myself and how I made decisions. As an eyewitness to my children's lives, I could see how what they believed about themselves influenced their decisions. When the world told them they were ugly, annoying, stupid, or unwanted, I wanted to shout out at the top of my lungs, "No, you are not! You are lovely, wanted, and treasured!" It frustrated me that some punk kid down the street had more credibility than I did. Then I thought about God as my Father. I thought about how the world had told me that I was worthless, unloved, and simply not enough—and how I had made decisions accordingly. I sought worth, love, and a life that would prove I was enough. Tenderly, God was shouting through Jesus, "You are worth it! You are loved...and I am enough!" This was the "Aha" moment that changed everything.

When we receive God's identity for us (and believe it), we experience freedom. Suddenly, the opinions of the world and those around us pale in comparison to the voice of our Father. As we live in our identity, seeking to live out the life we were created to live in Christ, then we can genuinely ask the next question: "Who did God create my child to be?" It is here that we begin to understand the Father's heart for spiritual parenting. This is often a difficult posture for us as moms.

We may believe intellectually that our children belong to God and that they were created for His glory, but daily living can tempt us to believe that they were created to reflect us instead of the Father. I can remember thinking and even saying to my children, "Don't do this or that because you will embarrass me in front of my friends or family members." In that sentence, I am communicating to my child that she is a reflection of me and that it is her job to bring me acclaim or not cause me shame.

How arrogant of me! Instead, from the beginning, we ought to see our children as image-bearers of God for His glory. Each of us was created in God's image. We bear His fingerprint—and no two are alike. At the end of our season of parenting, don't we ultimately want our children to look like Christ? That is a much higher goal than trying to keep our children from embarrassing us in public!

Questions to Ponder

- In what ways do you need to repent from the temptation to create and mold your child into your own image?
- How can you practically "die to yourself" and to your personal ambitions for your child and sincerely seek God every day, asking Him to reveal His plan for him/her?
- Why do you think you may fail to recognize, on any given day, God's incredible plan for your child's life? Why do you sometimes miss out on seeing this contribution He wants him/her to play in His story?

Faith-Filled Ideas

Here are two ideas that helped me as a young mom to help my children understand their identity in Christ:

1. Bless your children with this simple blessing:
   [Insert your child's name], may you know that the God who chose you before the creation of the world, loves *you*. He knows you. He cares for you, has a plan for your life, and wants to be close to you. May you always remember that no matter what you experience in this world, God will always be on your side because you belong to Him.

2. Create an acronym using the letters of your child's name and give each letter a word that "identifies" your child. After creating it, share why you chose each word and place it in a prominent spot in your home where your child will see it.

_____

_____

journal

_____
_____
_____
_____
_____
_____
_____
_____
_____
_____
_____
_____
_____
_____
_____
_____
_____
_____
_____
_____
_____
_____
_____
_____
_____
_____

> " Be very careful, then, how you live—not as unwise but as wise, making the most of every opportunity, because the days are evil. Therefore do not be foolish, but understand what the Lord's will is. "
>
> ~ Ephesians 5:15-17

"The faith of children is most likely to grow when they have the opportunity to associate with adults who are growing persons who know and love God. The child's faith is inspired when he or she belongs to an inclusive community that seeks to live out God's love."
  ~ Catherine Stonehouse

- Today, as you consider how you are investing time in those who are like-minded and share your values and beliefs, ask the Holy Spirit to give you wisdom on how to cultivate a vibrant faith community around you and your children.
- Open your Bible and read Isaiah 40:29-31. Take some time to consider why we as moms (or our children) might become in need of renewed strength.

Creating an Environment of Faith Community

By: Dr. Michelle Anthony

It's imperative that we put our children in close proximity to the faith community, because the world is hostile toward their faith. They will need an intentional refuge and reprieve. They will need a place where they can take the pieces of their armor off and simply remember who they are...a moment where they are not the one who doesn't "fit in." In this place, they gain strength.

We must be wise to understand that our children will bear the marks of the world's harsh conditions, and therefore we must make provisions for a different kind of community, a community of refuge. I've had to consider in each season of my children's lives what this would look like: participation in worship on Sunday, involvement in small groups during the week, rearranging summer plans for camp or mission trips, bringing mentors into our spiritual family, and sacrificing to make community happen in our home. We intentionally focused on these things in order to make them happen. How would we spend our money in order to accomplish these things? What luxuries or entitlements would we need to sacrifice in order to re-prioritize what is most important? These types of decisions had to be made swiftly and with intentionality; otherwise, the opportune times we had been given would have evaporated without us even noticing!

Ask yourself right now, "How will I intentionally and strategically set up an environment where my children will be a part of a vibrant faith community?" Isaiah 40:29-31 describes how those who wait upon the Lord will mount up with wings like eagles. This word picture of soaring, of being carried by the wind, makes me think of the freedom and perspective we would experience by flying in such a manner, in contrast perhaps to a hummingbird that flutters her wings, toils, strives, and flies so close to the ground that she can't have the bigger perspective on life.

The faith community offers this freedom and perspective to our children. Our children learn what it means to "wait on the Lord" together with others. They learn what it means to live by faith instead of sight and to gain an eternal perspective. They are prayed for. They learn about God's Word. They experience God Himself, and others are there to testify that the experiences are real. They need all of these things, just like the Old Testament children whose annual feasts offered them strength for the days ahead when they felt alone and depleted of hope. The world acts as a leech on our children's hearts and souls, and none are unscathed by it. Yet, the community of faith was designed by God to pour into and build up our children in ways that support us as mothers.

Questions to Ponder

- What circumstances play into "going it alone" without the support of like-minded believers?
- What sacrifices will you or your family need to make in order to make your faith community or church a bigger priority?
- Identify some practices and/or people that will encourage your commitment to being a part of a vibrant community of believers that will impact your children's lives.

Faith-Filled Ideas

Here are some ideas that helped me as a young mom keep my faith community a priority amidst all the other demands on my time/attention:

1. If you are not involved in a local church, start looking today. Ask friends for suggestions. Determine to not just "attend" but get involved (especially in your child's class). The enemy will tell you that you need a "break," but being involved is the only way to find true community.

2. Open your home for a women's Bible study or play group with other Christian women. Choose to share a least one prayer request each time you are together and pray for those needs.

3. Consider starting weekly or monthly "Sunday Suppers" with three to four other families. Take turns hosting and share a potluck style meal. Here you allow your children to play and build relationships outside of church in an intergenerational setting. This can become a rich tradition for many years that gives your child a sense of belonging and faith formation through sharing a meal, prayer, and godly conversation.

Start today, with an intentional plan of how you will redeem your time! God will renew you and your children in the presence of like-minded and strong believers.

journal

_____

_____

_____

_____

_____

_____

_____

journal

Food for the Soul

For me, in this crazy, busy season of life with my littles, showing love to my children comes down to 1 Corinthians 13:4. **Love. Is. Patient.** There it is, sweet and simple. God exhorts us to be patient. This verse really speaks to my heart because I allow my busyness to be an excuse for impatience with my children.

My three oldest kiddos are girls, and one thing they love to do is help mom in the kitchen. Having little helpers in the kitchen is hard when I am in a hurry and have other things I want to get done. Moms always have another chore to do, and it is tempting to believe that tasks are more important than children. They aren't. Slowing down and being present with our children nurtures them more than anything else we could do. Peacefully, joyfully spending time alongside them in work and play communicates love in a way that speaks to their hearts.

Here is a quick, easy, and kid-friendly granola bar recipe I make with my children. It can be customized to whatever flavors your kids or family prefer. We like to pick out different flavors each week. These granola bars are such a staple in our house, we make two batches at once. They are great for breakfast or an on-the-go snack when you want something quick.

EASY GRANOLA BARS By: Brandi Carson

Ingredients:

3 cups old-fashioned oats
1 can sweetened condensed milk
¼ teaspoon salt

⅓ cup wheat germ or ground flax seed (optional)
⅓ cup sliced almonds (optional)
½ – 1 cup flavorings
Non-stick cooking oil spray

Flavor Options:

- peanut butter
- chocolate chip and peanut butter
- honey
- pumpkin, cinnamon, and/or chocolate chips
- cinnamon raisin or mixed fruit

- coconut
- coconut chocolate chip
- chocolate chip
- chocolate (1 tablespoon cocoa powder)
- or any other flavors you like

Directions:

1. Preheat oven to 350 degrees.

2. Mix all ingredients together thoroughly. If using peanut butter, melt in microwave for a few seconds. Let cool before adding any chocolate chips, if using.

3. Spray a 9×13 pan with non-stick cooking oil spray.

4. Pour mixed filling in the pan. Wet hands and press firmly down (like you would with rice crispy treats).

5. Bake for 20-22 minutes. Let cool and cut into 16-24 bars.

6. Store in the refrigerator for up to two weeks, if they last that long!

Spiritual Parenting

~ Week Four ~

Dear Mama,

What does it mean to be a spiritual parent? It means taking upon ourselves the God-given mandate to train our children to know God, to follow His precepts, and to trust His plans wholeheartedly. Sounds simple enough in theory, but if you're like me, that feels like an overwhelming task most days—especially when our own faith feels so weak at times. Thankfully, in our weakness, He is strong (Romans 8:26, 1 Timothy 1:12, 2 Corinthians 12:9). He is more than enough for us, so it's not our job to worry about tomorrow; it's our job to trust in our Heavenly Father!

So, practically, what does this look like? Mama, your relationship with God is your highest priority. Just as you cannot drive your minivan with an empty fuel tank, you cannot—cannot—raise your children with an empty spiritual tank. In Genesis, we read that Adam and Eve walked in the Garden with God, communing constantly with the loving Father who created them in order to have relationship with them. Friend, we were created for relationship with God—continual companionship with the God of the universe. God desires our presence. He desires our reliance. He desires our communion. Only with time spent walking with God through worship, prayer, Bible study, and fellowship with our spiritual community, will we be filled in order to pour into the lives of each of our children.

And, if doubt tries to sneak into your mind and heart, telling you that you cannot hear from God, or you cannot raise your children the way God intended, just think of *The Little Engine That Could*. Can I hear from God? "Yes, I can. Yes, I can. Yes, I can!" Has God empowered me to raise my children spiritually? "Yes, He has. Yes, He has. Yes, He has!" You were made for this, Mama!

Love,
Rebekah Measmer and the Help Club for Moms Team

> *So commit yourselves wholeheartedly to these words of mine...*
> *Teach them to your children. Talk about them when you are at home and when*
> *you are on the road, when you are going to bed and when you are getting up.*
> *Write them on the doorposts of your house and on your gates, so that*
> *as long as the sky remains above the earth, you and your children*
> *may flourish in the land the LORD swore to give your ancestors.*
>
> *~ Deuteronomy 11:18-21 (NLT)*

Mom Tips

By: Leslie Leonard

"Let your roots grow down into him, and let your lives be built on him. Then your faith will grow strong in the truth you were taught, and you will overflow with thankfulness." ~ Colossians 2:7 (NLT)

The Wise Woman Builds Her Spirit

- Ask yourself this question during your quiet time this week: "Am I actively depending on the Holy Spirit to guide me on my spiritual journey?" Journal your answer. Surrender and invite the Holy Spirit to take the lead.

- Read Proverbs 15:30. Write the verse in your journal. Take the words to heart and smile more during your everyday tasks.

The Wise Woman Loves Her Husband

- Pick a workout or exercise routine you can do together with your husband.

- Ask your husband to pray with you immediately after the children go to bed. It can be brief, especially if this is something new to you and your husband. If a child gets out of bed during your prayer time, instead of reprimanding, use the opportunity to model the importance of prayer together.

The Wise Woman Loves Her Children

- Buy some journals or notebooks for your kids to write down some Bible verses about growing in Christ. Have them draw pictures or paint in their journals about what they believe it means to have a relationship with God.

- Pick a verse for each of your children this week. Write these in a card for each of them and leave it on their bathroom mirror along with loving words of encouragement.

The Wise Woman Cares For Her Home

- What kind of home do you want to have? Do not think about the way you want your home to look but rather, how you want it to feel and how you want the Holy Spirit to be evident within the walls of your home. Do you want to fill your home with love, warmth, peace, worship, gentleness, thankfulness, self-sacrifice, unconditional love, generosity, and discipleship? Be intentional about building those qualities into your home life.

- Put away all of your winter clothing and accessories. Clean all the items and organize them by size, then donate or sell any unwanted items.

> 66 Be devoted to one another in love. Honor one another above yourselves.
> Never be lacking in zeal, but keep your spiritual fervor, serving the Lord. 99
> ~ Romans 12:10-11

"I will often be able to serve another simply as an act of love and righteousness... But I may also serve another to train myself away from arrogance, possessiveness, envy, resentment, or covetousness. In that case, my service is undertaken as a discipline for the spiritual life."
~ Dallas Willard

- Call your prayer partner for your 10-minute prayer call! Never underestimate the power of praying with a friend.

- Open your Bible and read Romans 12:1-2. Ponder this: the same word in the original language for service is also the same word for worship—*latria*. What an incredible thought! Paul, the original author, could not conceive of separating service and worship. They are one in the same in God's eyes. In light of this, how will you worship Him today?

Creating an Environment of Serving

By: Dr. Michelle Anthony

We all had chores growing up, right? I mean, every good home has some form of them. Let's face it, chores were a way to get things done and to help our parents out, but I wonder why have we for so many decades called this beautiful act of service a "chore?"

Think about the word "chore." It just sounds like a word that makes you want to groan. And we did, didn't we? When my parents told me I could play after I finished doing the laundry or the dishes, I simply wailed. I grumbled. I bargained. Anything but a chore! So when I became a mom, I had visions of children who would scurry about in joy, much like Cinderella's mice, knowing that the work just needed to be done. I envisioned them wanting to help out of the abundant gratitude in their hearts for all that we had provided for them.

Well, it didn't take long for that dream to be squelched. Innate in each of us is a bent toward selfishness. Instinctively, we know how to serve ourselves and eliminate all else from distracting us in this pursuit. We are not born servants. Most of us (if not all of us) just naturally come into this world saying, "Serve me." But you can cultivate an outward focus in your home by training this posture of the heart, from an early age, through the environment of service.

Creating an environment where your children ask, "What needs to be done?" is critical for their faith development. To have them walk into any room, situation, or relationship and ask this will change the way they see their world. It's a simple concept, but not one that comes naturally. This attitude must be cultivated in your children, and that will not happen unless you set out on an intentional course, making it a priority.

In my home, we chose not to have "chores." Well, actually we still implemented the concept, but instead of referring to them as chores, we decided to call them "acts of service." This might sound silly to you to think that we merely changed the name, but I wanted them to understand that what they were really doing was serving our family.

So we assigned designated areas of service to our children. My daughter had cleaning bathrooms, doing laundry, and washing dishes every other day, while my son had taking out the trash, mowing the grass, cleaning the spa, and washing dishes every other day. They needed to help with the groceries, the kitchen, the dog, the litter box, and their rooms, as needed. But I didn't want them to think of those things as a list to complete; rather, I wanted them to see our family as interdependent.

I remember the morning when I knew the idea was taking root. Around 6:30 a.m., I heard my son shouting in the hallway before school, "Mom! Chantel has not done her act of service, and now I don't have underwear for school." Although I then heard the argument that ensued as my daughter suggested that he was capable enough to wash his own underwear, I snuggled down in my bed with the satisfaction of knowing that not only had my son referred to the laundry as an "act of service," but also that both children saw how dependent they were upon each other for their needs to be met.

The apostle Paul said, "Be devoted to one another in brotherly love. Honor one another above yourselves. Never be lacking in zeal, but keep your spiritual fervor, serving the Lord" (Romans 12:10-11). Ultimately, when we serve each other, we are serving the Lord. Paul also writes in Philippians 2:3-4, "Do nothing out of selfish ambition or vain conceit, but in humility consider others better than yourselves. Each of you should look not only to your own interests, but also to the interests of others."

Additionally, one of the most important things that we can do as mothers is to recognize our own selfish bent. When we do, we will better understand why it's hard to give this type of heart to our children. It's difficult, and in fact, even impossible, to give away something we don't already have.

Questions to Ponder

- Where do you see selfishness in your life? In your family members' lives? How may you have represented service to one another in ways that are not acts of worship but rather chores to be dreaded? How can you change this perception?
- How can you see your service to your family as an act of worship to God?

Faith-Filled Ideas

Use dinnertime to ask, "How did you serve your family today?" On the occasion that your family has served one another, this will be a time of gratitude. On the occasion that your family has been more self-serving, this will be an opportunity to remind one another of the ways that you need each other.

journal

_____

_____

_____

_____

_____

journal

_____

_____

_____

_____

_____

_____

_____

_____

_____

_____

_____

_____

_____

_____

_____

_____

_____

_____

_____

_____

_____

_____

_____

_____

_____

_____

_____

> 66 No discipline seems pleasant at the time, but painful. Later on, however, it produces a harvest of righteousness and peace for those who have been trained by it. Therefore, strengthen your feeble arms and weak knees. Make level paths for your feet, so that the lame may not be disabled, but rather healed. 99
>
> ~ Hebrews 12:11-13

"That's how God chose to reveal to us the divine love, bring us back into an embrace of compassion, and convince us that anger has been melted away in endless mercy."

~ Henri Nouwen

- God is the perfect parent and because He loves us, He disciplines us. Before thinking about your role as a mom who disciplines her children, pause for a moment to think about your loving heavenly Father and your obedience to Him.

- Open your Bible and read Matthew 7:24-29. What do we know about why God requires complete obedience from us as His dear daughters?

Creating an Environment of Course Correction

By: Dr. Michelle Anthony

Disciplining our children is probably one of the most time—and energy—intensive aspects of a mom's daily life. Yet, how we discipline our children, and how that discipline reflects who God is, is supremely important. The answers to these questions make the role of parenting something we can't take lightly!

The author of Hebrews explains how course correction works in Hebrews 12:11-13. There is a greater goal than stopping bad behavior. It is found in the last word of verse 13: healing. The end goal for parents is to conduct God's discipline in such a way that our children experience healing from their sin. Few people will acknowledge feeling just as loved in their sin as they do in their success, but this is a biblical concept for those who are in Christ. Our standing with God is not shaken when we need correction; rather it is our heart that needs healing.

- **Step One: Discipline Must be Painful**

   Hebrews 12 outlines a three-step process for course correction. In verse 11, it says, "No discipline seems pleasant at the time, but painful." True healing starts with pain. So the first step is to determine what "pain" is for each child because each child is wired differently. Pain for one child is different from pain for another. But, Proverbs 22:6 urges us to "train up a child in the way he should go." As you take into account the personality and inner makeup of your child and how she responds to you and to circumstances, then you can identify what pain is for her. With God's help, you can adopt a child-specific discipline model.

• **Step Two: Build Them Up in Love**

The second stage comes from verse 12: "Strengthen your feeble arms and weak knees." Think about this for a minute. This is a word picture of arms and knees that have broken down. The parts of the body that allow us to move forward productively have gone limp.

So, in course correction, immediately after we bring the pain, we also bring restitution to that child in love, in reassurance, and in encouragement. It's important to note that the one who brings the pain must be the one who brings the love and encouragement.

This takes effort and practice. We need to learn the art of speaking to our children and not at them. They also need affection. We can hug our children, touch their shoulders or their legs—something physical to tell them they are loved.

• **Step Three: Make a Straight and Level Path**

The third step in God's plan for course correction is stated in Hebrews 12:13: "'Make level paths for your feet,' so that the lame may not be disabled, but rather healed." Making a level path for our children's feet simply involves plotting out the new course for them. Here we teach them what it means to change and acknowledge that they will need God's help to do this.

Making a level path is telling them you have an idea of how they can navigate differently should the experience arise again, and then walking through those steps. This is where God can use our wisdom gained from having lived and made our own mistakes. We share ourselves with our children candidly.

Questions to Ponder

• Which of these three steps is most difficult? Why?

• Have you fallen into the trap of good cop/bad cop with your spouse, if you are married? If you are single, does the weariness cause you to become more strict or more lenient?

• In what ways do you want to discipline similarly or opposite to how you were disciplined as a child? Why?

Faith-Filled Ideas

Here are a couple of practical ideas that might help you to view course correction as a reflection of God's love instead of something that is draining you each day:

1. Seek a child-specific "pain" (write down for each child what is painful for him/her), practice building your child up in love and affirmation immediately after the pain so that they equate the two as going together, and don't forget to give specific words of encouragement to set forth a straight path for her to walk in. Reward or recognize when this path is chosen.

2. Play a "course correction" game with your young children where you give them two options of a path to take. You can place two divergent paths on the floor with colored paper or pillows. One path leads to peace and righteousness with God and the other path leads to pain and sadness. Give illustrations of situations where your children have a choice. Have them keep making good or bad choices until they reach the pain or the joy. Celebrate when they make good choices and talk through the ramifications of the poor choices.

3. Read Matthew 7:24-29 and explain how the person who heard the words and obeyed was like the man who built his house on the rock and the one who heard the words and did not obey was like the man who built his house on the sand. Describe or show (object lesson style) how building on a rock is much better and safer than building on the sand.

Don't give up. It's a training process. Today as you listen to God about the issues deep in your children's hearts, make yourself available to the wisdom in Hebrews 12:11-13.

Journal

> ❝ Follow God's example, therefore, as dearly loved children and
> walk in the way of love, just as Christ loved us and gave himself up for us
> as a fragrant offering and sacrifice to God. ❞
> ~ Ephesians 5:1-2

*"The best things your children will learn about God will be from watching you
try to find out for yourself. Jesus said, 'Seek and you will find.' They will not
always do what you tell them to do, but they will be—good and bad—as they
see you being. If your children see you seeking, they will seek—the finding
part is up to God."*
  ~ Polly Berrien Berends

• Open your Bible and read about how Jesus follows what His Father does in
  John 5:19-20. How does this passage help us understand our role with our
  heavenly Father and our role as models for our children to follow?

Creating an Environment of Modeling

By: Dr. Michelle Anthony

One of my favorite things about children is how they mimic almost anything or anyone with great precision. When my kids were little, I marveled at how they could imitate anyone from pop singers to cartoon characters. It was especially funny when one of them candidly imitated a family member, exposing their bad behavior and in effect, saying what we all wanted to say but couldn't.

However, it wasn't as funny when that child mimicked something unpleasant that I had modeled by my actions. Once, upon correction, my daughter reminded me she was only doing what she had just witnessed me doing. She was right. I had been caught.

I realized very quickly that raising children was like holding up a very large and animated mirror—and sometimes I didn't like what I saw! You see, there are times when we don't even realize the things we are passing down to our children just because they live among us and learn from us in every one of life's situations.

Some of these things are commendable. For instance, my husband and I have passed down to our children an ability to interact with people of diverse ages, races, and cultures. I also modeled how to keep a clean room by making my bed every morning and picking up the house before going to bed. Yet other things I've modeled are not so praiseworthy. I seem to consistently run about five to ten minutes late. I don't like this about myself, and today, I try to be prompt. But as a young mom I modeled being late and not making time a priority. As a result, my daughter has struggled with this same issue, and it pains me to see her dealing with something that has been hard for me. My husband has a tendency to deal impatiently with the imperfect drivers on the highway, and my son, when he acquired his own license to drive, seemed to share this same frustration. Perhaps this characteristic in children is why Paul said, "Be imitators of God, therefore, as dearly loved children" (Ephesians 5:1). He knew the nature of children to imitate and desired that this would be our posture before our heavenly Father. Imitating God is always a good thing. He is perfect. I can't fail when I choose to behave the way Christ modeled for us. Yet as a parent, I am a frail and tainted example of that. My children will mimic me. And whether I like it or not, I am the primary role model in their lives during the most formative years.

Understanding the role I play is critical to me as I model not only life here in this world, but also what it means to live for a world to come. I have to ask myself, "What kinds of things do I want my kids to imitate?" Even Jesus said, "I only do the things that I see my Father doing" in John 5:19. If Jesus chose to obey the Father and to follow in step with everything He saw His Father doing or being, we too ought to endeavor to live our lives in the same manner. When we do this, then we can say to our children what Paul said to his disciples, "You are to imitate me, just as I imitate Christ" (I Corinthians 11:1).

So how do we do these things? I believe we do them by abiding in Christ and allowing His Spirit to guide our lives. These are the two main processes of spiritual growth. In any relationship, as we grow to know and understand the person we love, we grow in our understanding of how to best respond to him/her. The Christian life is all about responding to God. From the moment we choose to surrender our lives to God and accept the gift of salvation offered through Jesus, we begin the journey of relational transformation. We learn about who God is through His Word, and we choose to follow Jesus' example by praying and asking God's Spirit to give us the strength to do what His Word says. This type of dependence in prayer, in the Bible, and upon His Spirit (instead of our own fortitude) gives us the ability to model a life that has been surrendered to God for His glory—not our own.

Questions to Ponder

- Many things are "caught" and not "taught." What things are your children "catching" from watching you (both good and bad)?
- In what ways can you abide in Christ and learn from God's Word in ways that will allow you to "mimic" your heavenly Father?
- Identify some practices and/or people that will encourage your dependence upon the Holy Spirit both in the posture of your heart and the actions you implement.

Faith-Filled Ideas

Here are some ideas that helped me as a mom to be the best role model for my children:

1. Play games such as "Simon Says" or "Follow the Leader" with your children and then share with them how these games reflect how we are to always do what God says and that He will always be our leader to follow throughout all of our lives.

2. Take out several Bibles or Bible apps on a smartphone or computer and model to your children how to look up verses in the Bible. Show them how to do several and then let them try to find a few on their own.

journal

_____

_____

_____

_____

journal

Nurturing Your Child's Faith

By: Kathryn Egly

"Train up a child in the way he should go;
even when he is old he will not depart from it."
~ Proverbs 22:6 (ESV)

As parents, we are used to 'outsourcing' services for our kids. When we want them to learn to play the piano, we take them to a piano teacher. If we want them to learn Spanish, we take them to a Spanish class. When we want them to learn how to swim, we take them to swim lessons. And because we want our children to learn about Jesus and grow spiritually, we take them to church. We might be tempted to think, "Let's leave the teaching of spiritual matters to the professionals!"

But we can't outsource our children's spiritual development! We, as parents, spend more time with our children than the professionals. We know them best because we see them in their most vulnerable states—when they are angry, sad, hurting, lonely, curious, and sick. It is our role as parents to be the primary nurturers of our children's faith. Even if we don't feel equipped to teach about spiritual matters, our children will be impacted by the environment in our homes and the words we say or don't say.

Deuteronomy 6:6-9 (MSG) instructs us:

> Write these commandments that I've given you today on your hearts. Get them inside of you and then get them inside your children. Talk about them wherever you are, sitting at home or walking in the street; talk about them from the time you get up in the morning to when you fall into bed at night. Tie them on your hands and foreheads as a reminder; inscribe them on the doorposts of your homes and on your city gates.

Leading our children in a loving relationship with their Father God occurs in the natural flow of life— talking about it throughout the day, at bedtime, in the car, or on a walk. We must be intentional to live out our faith in our children's presence. They need to hear our prayers and our apologies. They need to know God is our Creator and Provider. They need to hear what He's done in our lives and how He's answered prayer. Spiritual development happens all the time, not just on Sunday mornings.

Raising our children is a big responsibility, but we have a *bigger* God who will empower us to be the mothers He has called us to be! The Bible tells us that the Holy Spirit is our Helper. The Holy Spirit will help us know how to teach and instruct our children:

> But the Helper will teach you everything. He will cause you to remember all the things I told you. This Helper is the Holy Spirit whom the Father will send in my name. (John 14:26 ICB)

The Bible also tells us that God will give us wisdom if we ask for it:

> But if any of you needs wisdom, you should ask God for it. God is generous. He enjoys giving to all people, so God will give you wisdom. (James 1:5 ICB)

Though passing on our faith is our responsibility, being a part of a local church can and should support us to "train up our children in the way that they should go" (Proverbs 22:6 ESV).

Your children were given to you from God, and He has equipped you to be the primary spiritual caregiver. Rely on Him to empower you!

journal

Creating a *Quiet Time* Basket

Why should you invest in creating a "Quiet Time" basket for your young children?

Teaching our young kids about Jesus, in the comfort of our homes, surrounded by love, could be some of the best Christian parenting we will ever do! It's amazing how God created our young ones to be little sponges. With their active imaginations, it's no wonder "childlike faith" is a coined term! Intentionally investing in your kids during this time could change the trajectory of their lives! Take 5-15 minutes per day to dig into this basket together. You child will enjoy time spent with you, and the nuggets of truth that they receve will be worth it!

What To Include In Your Basket

Children's Bible
Fun coloring crayons/colored pencils
Coloring books
Bible story picture books
Missionary stories for kids
Play-doh/kinetic sand
Snacks (only to be eaten during this time!)

He called a little child to him, and placed the child among them. And he said: "Truly I tell you, unless you change and become like little children, you will never enter the kingdom of heaven.
Matthew 18:2-3 (NIV)

For younger kids!

*** Color Printable found at myhelpclubformoms.com ***

Creating a *Quiet Time* Basket

Why should you invest in creating a "Quiet Time" basket for your pre-teen/teen?

Creating a spiritual discipline and love of learning about God's words and ways, is a beautiful seed to plant for you pre-teen or teenager. It will bless them for a lifetime! This does not need to be fancy, just filled with goodness! Sometimes, when we spend a little time making something special, our kids are more prone to do it or reach for it. Likewise, food makes everything better! Encourage your child to spend at least 5-10 minutes a day (morning or night), reading some items from their basket or journaling. You' may be surprised at how much they learn!

What To Include In Your Basket

Bible
Fun pens/pencils
Notebook for journaling
Scripture coloring book
Pre-teen/teen devotional
Snacks
Missionary stories/Inspirational books on following Jesus

For the word of God is alive and active. Sharper than any double-edged sword, it penetrates even to dividing soul and spirit, joints and marrow; it judges the thoughts and attitudes of the heart.
Hebrews 4:12 (NIV)

For Pre-Teens & Teens!

Walking with John

Walking
with John
~ Week Five ~

"In the beginning was the Word, and the Word was with God, and the Word was God." ~ John 1:1

Precious Mama,

This week, we officially begin the Lenten season! It's the beautiful time of year when we intentionally carve out a few extra moments to ponder the life, death, and resurrection of our amazing Lord and Savior, Jesus Christ! We are so excited here at the Help Club for Moms to begin our journey together, "Walking with John," and learning more about the life of Jesus and His great love for us as we go.

For the next seven weeks, we invite you to join your Help Club sisters around the world as we read the 21 chapters of John together and soak in the wide, long, high, and deep love of Jesus Christ. The love of Jesus is so great that we even have to pray to understand it!

During the "Walking with John" study, we encourage all of our moms to not only read the three Bible study devotions each week but also to carve out a few moments to watch the correlating chapter in the movie *Life of Jesus: Gospel of John* by the Jesus Film Project. This amazing dramatization of the book of John is separated into chapters for easy viewing. Since the movie is word-for-word Scripture, it provides an even clearer picture and understanding of how Jesus lived and loved.

The movie is available for free through the YouVersion Bible App under *videos*. You can buy the movie on Amazon or watch it for free with an Amazon Prime membership. On YouTube, you can find it separated out into 21 videos. Look for *The Gospel of John Chapter by Chapter*. This movie is a great investment in the spiritual life of your family. I have purchased at least five copies! Be sure to watch the videos with all of your children who are elementary-age and older. They need to ponder Jesus during Lent too!

We are so excited to hear how this season encourages you in your walk with Jesus! We are praying for you!

Love,
Deb Weakly and the Help Club For Moms Team

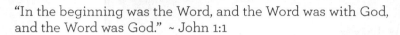 *The plainest reason why the Son of God is called the Word seems to be, that as our words explain our minds to others, so was the Son of God sent in order to reveal his Father's mind to the world.*
~ Matthew Henry

Mom Tips

By: Leslie Leonard

*"Let your roots grow down into him, and let your lives be built on him.
Then your faith will grow strong in the truth you were taught,
and you will overflow with thankfulness."*
~ Colossians 2:7 (NLT)

The Wise Woman Builds Her Spirit

• Choose to speak with kindness at least one day this week. Season your words with grace, especially if you feel frustrated or angry. Be an example for your children by responding with a soft, gentle answer.

• Choose to give up or fast from one pleasure this week.

The Wise Woman Loves Her Husband

• Ask your husband to teach you something he's good at doing.

• Declare a "No TV Night" one day this week. After you put the kids to bed, turn off the television, and spend some time talking, playing a board game, or relaxing with one another.

The Wise Woman Loves Her Children

• Go on a family walk after dinner one night this week.

• Help your children memorize Colossians 3:12. Write it on your chalkboard or bathroom mirror. Use this verse to teach your little ones that choosing to be kind is always the right choice.

The Wise Woman Cares For Her Home

• Write two "thank you" or "just thinking of you" cards and send them in the mail this week.

• Spend some time sprucing up your yard with the kids. Pull weeds, trim trees and bushes, dispose of any trash, and maybe even have a family outing to pick out a new tree to plant.

> **The Word became flesh and made his dwelling among us. We have seen his glory, the glory of the one and only Son, who came from the Father, full of grace and truth.**
>
> ~ John 1:14

"Jesus Christ did not come into this world to make bad people good; He came into this world to make dead people live."
  ~ Lee Strobel

- Call your prayer partner for your 10-Minute prayer call! God is the one who has the power to work in your heart and the hearts of those you love. Prayer changes everything!

- Blessed is the name of the Lord! A day started out in devotion to God is sure to be a glorious one! Please gather your Bible and journal and find a quiet place in your home with no distractions.

- Read John 1:1-5, 12-14, and 29-30. If you have time, however, reading all of John 1 is encouraged. This is such a foundational chapter of the Bible and you won't be disappointed in taking the time to read it. Write verse 14 in your journal and memorize it.

Jesus is the Light of the World

By: Rachel Jones

Jesus is light and He is full of grace and truth. He came for each and every one of us and He did it gladly. I would love to share with you the happy song from page 200 of *The Jesus Storybook Bible*:

> Because God loves us with a never stopping, never giving up, unbreaking, always and forever love—Heaven is breaking through! He is sending us a Light from Heaven to shine on us like the sun, to shine on those who live in darkness and in the shadow of death, to guide our feet into the way of peace.

Wow! That is our Jesus. Because of God's unrelenting love for His people, He sent Jesus to be in the flesh and make His dwelling among us (John 1:14). Jesus became the bridge for us to get to the Father!

I am so grateful for my Savior, Jesus Christ, and the incomparable priceless gift of forgiveness He gave me by grace, through faith in His atoning blood. His sacrifice brings hope for redemption to those who repent and believe.

As Easter approaches, how are we going to teach our children this most significant truth? God has given our children to us for a time, and it is our duty and privilege to impart to them the importance of the death and resurrection of Jesus.

I am so excited to share with you mamas some amazing ideas I have found for having a Christ-centered Easter in our homes.

Easter Jelly Bean Prayer Envelopes
This is a cute, tangible reminder of why we celebrate Easter. My girls love making these and giving them out as gifts to our family, friends, and neighbors. Here is an informative link explaining everything (with a free printable): http://www.theidearoom.net/easter-jelly-bean-prayer-envelopes

Passover-Inspired Easter Dinner

How about changing your traditional Easter brunch/dinner to a Passover or Last Supper-inspired meal? Even though Jesus ate this meal with His disciples the night before His death, making it on Easter Sunday is a great tradition and a very special way to honor Him. Your kids will not forget this extraordinary night! Here is a link with a menu and lots of details: https://fhelessons.wordpress.com/2013/03/11/passover-inspired-easter-dinner/

Christ-Centered Easter-Egg Hunt

I love this idea so much! Easter egg hunts are such a fun part of the holiday when you have young kids at home, but why does every single egg have to be filled with only candy?! Adding some Scripture on small pieces of paper along with the candy points the day back to Jesus. While your kids are enjoying one of their pieces of chocolate, you or your husband can read aloud some of the most important verses from the Bible about Jesus' amazing sacrifice. http://www.messestomemories.com/2015/03/christ-centered-easter-egg-hunt.html

Science Experiment: Jesus Washes our Sins Away

As a homeschooler, this idea caught my eye immediately! Young children who enjoy hands-on projects will really enjoy this. This object lesson will also help your kids better understand what Jesus did and still does for all of us. https://www.icanteachmychild.com/science-experiment-jesus-washes-our-sins-away/

A Sense of the Resurrection Book

At The Help Club for Moms, we have loved the book, *Truth in the Tinsel* for a few years. This priceless book guides parents in sharing the miracle of Christmas with their children. And did you all know that the same author has an Easter counterpart?! *A Sense of the Resurrection* contains 12 activities for families to put themselves right where Jesus was when He laid down His life for us. This is a must own if you have young kids! https://truthinthetinsel.com/shop/a-sense-of-the-resurrection-ebook/

Questions to Ponder

• How can you keep the focus on Jesus, our Messiah this Easter? Is there anything in your Easter celebration detracting from the holiday? Maybe it is a family tradition or a new activity that doesn't glorify the Lord or is simply a waste of time. This may seem harsh, but it is always a good idea to re-evaluate how you are doing things as a mother. I have had to look closely at our holiday traditions over the years. Every time I have remained true to the Lord, my family has had a special time of blessing.

• How can you make this Easter more memorable for your children? What one thing would you want your children to remember the most about Easter? How are you setting an example in this area?

Faith-Filled Ideas

If your children are old enough, I would like to encourage you to involve them in the planning! The older siblings will love helping mom in preparing some of these activities for their younger siblings.

Read 1 Peter 2:24-25 with them, rejoicing in the healing wounds of Christ on the cross. Finally, as you pray together, "give your bodies to God because of all he has done for you. Let them be a living and holy sacrifice—the kind he will find acceptable" (Romans 12:1 NLT).

Journal

Walking with John

"Sometimes we know what we have to do but we lack the courage to do it. Let us learn from Mary how to make decisions, trusting in the Lord."
~ Pope Francis

- It's your time to dive into God's Word and ponder the things of Jesus! Take a few seconds to clear your mind and heart, and be ready to hear what He has for you today, friend.
- Read all of John Chapter 2. After you have finished, go back and reread verses 1-5. Let's begin!

Believing for Miracles

By: Krystle Porter

I am always impressed by Mary, the mother of Jesus. Her love for God and His Son was evident in her steadfast commitment to Jesus. From the moment the angel appeared telling her that she would carry Jesus in her womb, to His gruesome death on the cross, Mary accepted her role in God's plan. I absolutely love Mary's response in Luke 2:18-19 when the shepherds found the baby Jesus with Mary and Joseph, and recounted their visit from an angel: "And all who heard it wondered at what the shepherds told them. But Mary treasured up all these things, pondering them in her heart."

With that in mind, let's jump in to our reading from John 2. Jesus is much older now, but we see his mom is still by his side, at a wedding with Jesus and his disciples. The thirsty guests had finished off all the wine at the party. Without hesitation, Mary knew what to do; ask Jesus for help. She was so confident He could solve the problem, she told the servants, "Do whatever he tells you."

My first thought as I read this chapter was to focus on the miracle of Jesus turning the water into wine, which is truly incredible and awe-inspiring. But at second glance, Mary was the one I was drawn to. She knew exactly what to do. She knew that Jesus was the answer. Her faith was so certain, she convinced the servants to obey Jesus!

Mary believed in miracles before they came to be. She trusted Jesus; who He was and what He came to do. After all, she carried this baby in her womb and *knew* Him deeply.

Think about that, mama. She knew Jesus just like you know your own sweet children—the wrinkles of His little hands after birth, the birthmarks on His body, His cry, His funny expressions, little quirks—they became a part of her. As Jesus' mother, Mary knew the Savior intimately, as you know your children in a way few people can. You may even be able to predict their behavior in certain situations, right?

This causes me to step back and glean whatever I can from a woman who knew Jesus in this unique way. I trust Mary, just as I would a dear friend, to have unique insight into her child. This mama, knew that her miraculous boy could perform miraculous works. And that's what He did.

Do you need a miracle in you life today, mama? Do you need to be inspired by Mary to believe in a miracle before it has come to pass? Jesus breathed words of life into the writers of each book of the Bible, so it can penetrate through time to reach us today. This story of Jesus changing the water to wine and the mother who knew He would do it beforehand, was not written by accident. It was meant to speak to our hearts!

Friends, let's be women who *believe in miracles before they come to pass*. Let's trust this fellow mama, to tell us what is true about our Savior!

Questions to Ponder

- Is there a place in your life where you need a miracle? Write down a couple of things that God brings to your mind.

- Have you ever believed that God would work a miracle before it has happened? Why or why not? Take some time to consider what it would be like and how it would change your faith if you did!

Faith-Filled Ideas

Underneath what you wrote down for places you need a miracle, write these words: "I believe Jesus is going to work a miracle in this!"

Take a few minutes to pour your heart out to God. Tell Him that you trust His kindness toward you. Tell Him that you believe He is a miracle worker. Tell Him that you trust His perfect timing. Think about each of the situations where you need a miracle and imagine Jesus sweeping in and making it come to reality. Experience the joy that comes from believing in God's favor toward you!

Walking with John

journal

_____

_____

_____

_____

_____

_____

_____

_____

_____

_____

journal

Walking with John

"When I came with open hands and an open heart to see if God could actually speak for Himself, I realized how much baggage I had heaped upon the Bible and how much hearsay I had believed about God."
~ Brian Hardin, *Reframe*

- Today, as we prepare for Resurrection Sunday, let's dive into the deep questions of life and eternity. Whether your faith is secure or needing encouragement, read the entirety of John chapter 3 and we'll study together. Take notes or highlight any part that sticks out to you.

The Beginning of a New Story

By: Tara Fox

As a young child, life is an endless novel full of hope with pages yet to be turned. With age comes the understanding that this book is a fast read. Even if it's a very long story, every book has a last page.

On one thing we can all agree; earthly death is certain. What then? John chapter 3 speaks candidly on the subject of death and what happens after we close the book of our earthly existence. John juxtaposes these spiritual basics: faith in Jesus leads to eternal life and rejecting Jesus leads to eternal death. If this doesn't line up with your beliefs, you may find a key to what's missing ahead.

Nicodemus lived his life as a devout religious Pharisee, but felt a pull to something more. Under the cover of night (not to be found out by his community), he went to visit Jesus. He couldn't help but notice there was something different about Him. As a Jew, he understood that if Jesus was performing miracles, He must have been a teacher *from* God.

The part Nicodemus could not wrap his mind around was that Jesus *is* God; fully God, fully man. Paul explains the deity of Jesus in Philippians:

> Though he was God, he did not think of equality with God as something to cling to. Instead, he gave up his divine privileges; he took the humble position of a slave and was born as a human being. When he appeared in human form, he humbled himself in obedience to God and died a criminal's death on a cross. (Philippians 2:6-8 NLT)

The Jews had watched and waited for centuries for their Savior. And yet, the Jewish nation rejected their prophesied Savior, Yeshua, even as He lived and proclaimed His divinity right before their very eyes. Jesus looked different from what they expected. God coming to earth in the form of man offended their preconceived notions and just didn't make sense. As Nicodemus conversed with Jesus, he tried to reconcile what was taught in His Jewish culture with the words of Jesus.

This is what many of us do. We come to God with so many questions and wrong beliefs, then walk away dissatisfied because we cannot make sense out of everything with our own human logic. With our inability to comprehend the deity of Jesus, the Holy Trinity, why God allows suffering, or any other reality we find hard to believe, we dismiss faith or put it off until we can "figure it out" on our own. These words spoken to Nicodemus changed everything for him: "I tell you the truth, unless you are born again, you cannot see the Kingdom of God" (John 3:3).

Wait, what? Did you catch that? Jesus says we cannot truly see or comprehend spiritual things unless we have accepted Christ and have been "born again" through the Spirit of God. Nicodemus tried to reason how this is possible using his human understanding. Jesus told him, "I assure you, we tell you what we know and have seen, and yet you won't believe our testimony. But if you don't believe me when I tell you about earthly things, how can you possibly believe if I tell you about heavenly things" (John 3:11-12 NLT)?

How about you: have you seen evidence of God working on earth? Have you heard testimonies of lives changed by knowing Jesus? Are you paying attention to biblical accounts? Have you looked around to see the undeniable, plain work of the Creator's hands? With all this evidence, does your mind still doubt? Just as we cannot see earthly things before we are born, we cannot see spiritual things until we are born in the Spirit. Come to Jesus with your questions. After all, He is "the author and finisher of our faith" (Hebrews 12:2).

Allow Jesus to meet you where you are as you follow Him each day of your life. As the creator of the universe, He has all the answers. You need never stop researching, asking, or realizing; you just get to do it with new eyes. The Bible tells us, if we need wisdom, all we need to do is ask God with faith in Him. Not only will He give us wisdom, he will not find fault for our asking.

> If you need wisdom, ask our generous God, and he will give it to you. He will not rebuke you for asking. But when you ask him, be sure that your faith is in God alone. Do not waver, for a person with divided loyalty is as unsettled as a wave of the sea that is blown and tossed by the wind. Such people should not expect to receive anything from the Lord. Their loyalty is divided between God and the world, and they are unstable in everything they do. (James 1:5-8 NLT)

John the Baptist sums up John chapter 3 so beautifully:

> The one who comes from above is above all; the one who is from the earth belongs to the earth, and speaks as one from the earth. The one who comes from heaven is above all. He testifies to what he has seen and heard, but no one accepts his testimony. Whoever has accepted it has certified that God is truthful. For the one whom God has sent speaks the words of God, for God gives the Spirit without limit. The Father loves the Son and has placed everything in his hands. Whoever believes in the Son has eternal life, but whoever rejects the Son will not see life, for God's wrath remains on them. (John 3:31-36)

When your faith is in Jesus, the last page of your book is really the beginning of a new story! Come to Jesus! He is waiting with open arms.

Questions to Ponder
• Who is Jesus to you?

• Do you know if you will be spending eternity in heaven or hell?

• With whom is God prompting you to share this message?

Faith-Filled Ideas
Tell Jesus you are ready to put your faith in Him if you haven't already. Find a church to attend that lines up with the Word of God. Share your decision to follow Jesus with another mature Christian and tell someone at the Help Club for Moms!

Walking with John

Share your testimony with your children. Ask them if they have put their faith in Jesus. If so, help them prepare their own testimony to share.

When teaching or discussing theology with your children, show them throughout the Bible God's plan to save sinners. Emphasize God's great love for them and His desire to have a relationship with them.

Journal

_____

_____

_____

_____

_____

_____

_____

_____

_____

_____

_____

_____

_____

_____

_____

_____

_____

_____

_____

_____

_____

_____

_____

Walking with John

What is Lent?

For Kids!

Walking with John

Lent is a time of preparation for Easter, the Christian holiday that celebrates the resurrection of Jesus Christ.

Suggest that your child think about Lent as a way to get closer to God. Point out that Jesus used his forty days to get away from distractions and be with God. Tell you son or daughter that they can benefit from Lent by pushing aside at least some of the distractions of the world.

Tell your child that Lent lasts for forty days because that's how long Jesus wandered in the desert, fasting, while He resisted Satan's temptations. Explain that your child has an opportunity, during the forty days of Lent, to be like Jesus! They too can resist temptations and use this time to become closer to God.

Read Psalm 103:11-12

Read Mark 1:13

*** Color Printable found at myhelpclubformoms.com ***

Create a
Lenten Prayer Station
at Home

How do you create the space to journey through Lent in a meaningful way as a family?

Create a Lenten Prayer Station!

Here are some ideas for what you can place at your station:

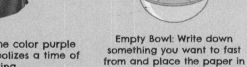

Candle: Always a symbol of God's presence with us.

Purple Cloth: The color purple during lent symbolizes a time of waiting.

Empty Bowl: Write down something you want to fast from and place the paper in the bowl.

Cross: Take time to look at the cross together and talk about the Crucifixion and the Resurrection.

Scripture: The Good Shepherd of Psalm 23 is a wonderful image to meditate on with young children.

*** Color Printable found at myhelpclubformoms.com ***

Easter is just around the corner. For many, the Easter holiday means family gathering together to celebrate Christ's ultimate sacrifice and resurrection. If your family is anything like mine, food is usually involved! Whether it is a big, fancy meal, potluck, or just snack-type foods, I have an excellent recipe for you: Meatballs.

These meatballs are so versatile. They can be used in many different types of recipes and with a wide variety of sauces, are great as an appetizer or even a main meal, and can easily feed a crowd. The best part about meatballs is that they are so incredibly simple to make. I often make huge batches when I find ground beef and/or Italian sausage on sale. I bake them and freeze them as an easy go-to meal on a busy night.

MEATBALL APPETIZER

By: Brandi Carson

<u>Ingredients</u>:

1 pound Italian sausage

1 pound ground beef or ground turkey

2 eggs, whisked

½ cup breadcrumbs

1 teaspoon salt and pepper

½ cup grated Parmesan cheese

<u>Directions</u>:

1. Preheat oven to 375 degrees.

2. In a large bowl, combine all ingredients.

3. Using your hands, mix until all meat, egg, and seasoning is well combined.

4. Using two spoons or a mini "ice-cream" scoop, make mini meatballs. Scoop 1"– 1 ½ " balls and place on a pre-sprayed sheet pan. Wet hands and roll the meat into balls.

5. Bake meatballs for 12-15 minutes until brown and cooked through.

Your meatballs are now ready for the freezer or whatever delicious recipe you choose!

Walking with John

~ Week Six ~

Dear Sister in Christ,

Welcome to the second week of Lent! There is no better way to grow in our faith, or in our relationship with the Lord Jesus Christ, than to read His Word every day. Romans 10:17 says, "...faith comes from hearing the message, and the message is heard through the word about Christ." As we read the book of John, we get to know who Jesus Christ is. We find out He is the Bread of Life (chapter 6) and He is the Living Water (chapter 4). When we eat this bread and drink His Living Water, we will never be thirsty again. Jesus says, "The water I give (you) will become in (you) a spring of water welling up to eternal life" (John 4:14).

Are you hungry? Are you thirsty? Have you been trying to fill the void in your life with the pleasures of this world or with material possessions that will rot and rust? God's Word says: "...man does not live on bread alone but on every word that comes from the mouth of the LORD" (Deuteronomy 8:3). Fill your mind daily with the Word of God. Read your Bible, listen to sermons and biblical podcasts, and play praise and worship music as you walk through your day. Your faith in Christ will surely grow!

The things of this Earth will pass away but Jesus Christ and his kingdom will last forever. The things of God are the things that matter in this life. I encourage you to turn to Jesus. Learn to abide in Him and His Word. Drink His living water and you will never be thirsty again.

With love and prayers,
Jennifer Valdois and the Help Club For Moms Team

> *She was willing to settle for less. Jesus wanted to give her more.*
> *While she was happy with temporal satisfaction—*
> *a drink of tepid water from a well in the desert—*
> *Jesus longed for her to experience eternal joy.*
> ~ *Liz Curtis Higgs*

Mom Tips

By: Leslie Leonard

"Let your roots grow down into him, and let your lives be built on him. Then your faith will grow strong in the truth you were taught, and you will overflow with thankfulness." ~ Colossians 2:7 (NLT)

The Wise Woman Builds Her Spirit

- Plan a date with friends such as a fun girls night out or in. Invite someone new who might need a friend.

- Is there anything you can clear from your schedule this week? Ask for the Holy Spirit's guidance in planning your time and activities this week.

The Wise Woman Loves Her Husband

- Happily greet your husband as he walks in the door from work every day this week. Give him a few minutes to collect his thoughts and leave the workday behind before asking him to help you with the house or children.

- Get up early this week to make your husband breakfast before he heads to work. If he is not a breakfast eater, make a pot of coffee. Share some quiet together time, and send him off with a smile.

The Wise Woman Loves Her Children

- Smile as much as you can at your kids this week. Post reminders in your house, car, and on your phone.

- Give your kids some cheap terracotta pots and paint to create their own planters. Combine a few packs of random seeds, then plant them in their decorated pots. Let your kids have fun taking care of them and being surprised by what grows. Use this fun craft to discuss biblical analogies about soil, seeds, pruning, harvesting, etc.

The Wise Woman Cares For Her Home

- Spend time this week cleaning out *that* drawer in your kitchen. We all have one; the dreaded "junk drawer." Inventory the contents, throw away any garbage, and move items to their proper homes.

- Know what you will serve for dinner by 9:00 am for three days this week. Remember to defrost any meat and prep any vegetables ahead of time.

<blockquote>
❝ Jesus replied, 'If you only knew the gift God has for you and who you are speaking to, you would ask me, and I would give you living water.' ❞

~ John 4:10 (NLT)
</blockquote>

"The overwhelming, never-ending, reckless love of God. It chases me down, fights 'til I'm found, leaves the ninety-nine. I couldn't earn it, and I don't deserve it, still, You give Yourself away."
~ Cory Asbury, *Reckless Love of God*

Walking with John

- Call your prayer partner and pray together, asking for the Holy Spirit to guide you through your week.

- Friends, Jesus is fighting for you; He loves you dearly and chases you down whenever you turn from Him. It defies logic, really. He is the one bearing the immensely, unfathomably perfect gift, and yet *He* relentlessly pursues *us*. Turn to God today and see what happens. Invite God into your heart and your life and accept the peace and joy that follow!

- Read the story of Jesus with the woman at the well: John 4:1-42. Write verse 10 in your journal.

Come as You Are

By: Heather Doolittle

Are you praying for a loved one who is living a life of emptiness, sin, and discontent? Or are you curious about God but just can't get past the harsh condemnation attributed to the Church? If so, continue reading. God wants us all to come to Him, and He is not scared away by our sin or scars. If He were, no one would be saved because not one of us is truly worthy of His unfailing love. "For all have sinned and fall short of the glory of God" (Romans 3:23 NKJV). The story of Jesus with the woman at the well in John 4 reminds us of this truth, as Jesus demonstrates his love and grace as well as a beautiful display of evangelism at its best. Here, Jesus models God's perfect love and shows us Christ-followers how to draw others to God through that love.

You see, Jesus offered this woman eternal salvation, knowing that she was no typical, up-standing Israelite. She was a Samaritan (strike one), she'd had five divorces (strike two), and she lived with her boyfriend (strike three). Any one of these failings would have rendered her unworthy of speaking with a Jewish teacher back then, and she had the trifecta. She pointed this out to Jesus (at least the first strike) when He approached her and asked for water: "Then the woman of Samaria said to Him, 'How is it that You, being a Jew, ask a drink from me, a Samaritan woman?' For Jews have no dealings with Samaritans" (John 4:9 NKJV).

Since this woman was an easy target for judgment and criticism, I suspect her response was not a display of respect, but her snarky way of refusing Him. That's not a wise way to talk to the King of Kings, but Jesus' patient reply is the epitome of humility and grace. "If you knew the gift of God and who it is that asks you for a drink, you would have asked him and he would have given you living water" (John 4:10 NKJV). Since they were in a vast desert, this piqued her interest, and Jesus continued to tell her about His living water that never runs dry.

Lent ~ Week Six ~ Day Four

Jesus then mentioned the woman's husband, already knowing all about her complicated relationship status. Aside from proving His divine anointing, He was clarifying that God accepted her as-is, without stipulation. He was making certain she knew His invitation to living water and eternal life was not based on an erroneous first impression, intended for someone with a good, moral lifestyle. Jesus' magnificent invitation was for the real woman who stood before Him—sinful, lost, and broken. Jesus approaches all of us in the same manner: with an outstretched arm, freely offering His living water with grace, love, and forgiveness.

This Bible story is particularly close to my heart because it parallels my first life-changing encounter with Jesus. I became a Christian at the age of seven, in the sense that I believed God existed, but as I got older, my faith was too shallow to weather real trials. I searched for God but didn't find Him; Christianity seemed to me a list of rules, followed by inevitable failure, judgment, and condemnation. That wasn't something to which I wanted to devote my whole heart, and so I lived my life as I pleased, empty and longing for something deeper.

However, God wasn't content to leave our relationship at that. A couple of years into college, my boyfriend got me pregnant, which is a quick way to find yourself alone at a large party school. All around me, the message was that I should have an abortion—I screwed up and should cut my losses. I had a difficult enough time taking care of myself that I certainly couldn't give a child a good life. This worldly wisdom felt wrong, but I didn't have a clear vision for what was right. My salvation prayer went something like this: "*OK, God, I'll do this and see how it works out.*"

Then God met me in my day-to-day life, just as He did the woman at the well. He revealed His unconditional love through that precious baby and all the blessings that proceeded from a happy family and godly life. That unexpected baby and her loving father (now my husband) were God's perfect gift to me—a gift the world said I couldn't accept. The first time I looked into her sweet face, I felt an unconditional love that was new to me then, but has defined every day of my life since. God has revealed His love and grace to me in such a gentle way that He has won my whole heart. Why would I go back to an empty, sinful life when Jesus offers so much more? I suspect that after beginning to follow Jesus, the woman at the well asked the same question.

God does not require you to be sinless before He embraces you. He is prompting you to open your whole heart to love, releasing from it the accumulated unforgiveness, pain, and sin. Then the question changes from "why *stop* sinning?" to "why *keep* sinning?" Why would anyone want to sin and live in darkness when Jesus is willing to erase all sin and provide a better way? Those of us who, like the woman at the well, have experienced a life stuck in sin and bondage have no desire to go back there. Yes, everyone messes up, but God is interested in the intentions of our hearts, whether we embrace that sin or embrace Him. Obedience will follow (John 14:15).

Jesus didn't come to this woman to call her a sinner, which would be telling her what she already knew. Nor was He coming to offer salvation that would give her free rein to keep sinning. That would be as useless as planting a flower among a weed patch without removing the weeds that would choke it. Jesus came to *fulfill* the law and demonstrate its power and goodness by providing the "why," and then the "how." Jesus offers us a salvation that abolishes all sin and frees us from a life in bondage. He doesn't force us to be good; He frees us from evil so that we can be good.

Simply turn to God and ask for His free gift of living water. He will work out the rest as you walk with Him. "Ask and you will receive" (Matthew 7:7-8). What a powerful promise for all of us!

Questions to Ponder
• Have you run from God in any area of your life? Maybe it's as simple as neglecting to study the Bible regularly. Repent and ask God to help you follow Him more closely.

Walking with John

- Have you accepted Jesus into your heart and life? If not, pray this prayer from the Rev. Billy Graham and receive salvation and a new life in Christ Jesus:

  Dear Lord Jesus, I know that I am a sinner, and I ask for Your forgiveness. I believe You died for my sins and rose from the dead. I turn from my sins and invite You to come into my heart and life. I want to trust and follow You as my Lord and Savior. In Your Name.

- Did you pray this prayer? Email us at admin@helpclubformoms.com so we can prayer for you.

Faith-Filled Ideas

Live out God's goodness by modeling it to those around you, starting with your family. Forgive readily and respond kindly. When you neglect to do so, apologize (even if their bickering/ fighting/ whining/ temper tantrum brought on your outburst). Lead by example and be the change you want to see in your family. When other members of your family start to follow your example—if only for a moment—commend their kindness and thank them for it.

You can capture your husband's and children's hearts through unrelenting love and never-ending grace, just as Jesus showed us through this story and the entire Gospel.

journal

_____
_____
_____
_____
_____
_____
_____
_____
_____
_____
_____
_____
_____
_____
_____
_____

> Then Jesus said to him, 'Get up! Pick up your mat and walk.'
> At once the man was cured; he picked up his mat and walked.
>
> ~ John 5:8-9

"I hear You say,
'Come to the water
Come to the river
Come to the well
Come if you're thirsty
Come if you're broken
Come and be healed.'"
  ~ Kate Miner, *Come to the Water*

- Are you ready to witness another one of Jesus' miracles? Ask the Lord to calm everything inside you and all around you. Wait expectantly like a child to see the impossible take place.

- Read John 5.

Focus on the Miracles

By: Daphne Close

I think I might be a nitpicker. I remind my children to do their morning chores, but I don't affirm everything they accomplish. I only point out what they miss. Perhaps a better word to describe myself would be a perfectionist; or worse, a dictator!

Can you picture this man in John 5 who has been sick for thirty-eight years? We know very little about this man other than *nobody would help him*. Surely many people recognized this man who lay immobilized for decades. Therefore, it must have been quite obvious to see him walking around without a single ailment.

How would you have responded if you had witnessed this miracle? Would you have pointed him out to your friend? Would you have run up to him, hugged him, danced with him?

The Jewish leaders responded immediately. "You can't work on the Sabbath! The law doesn't allow you to carry that sleeping mat" (John 5:10 NLT)! They were so consumed with external obedience that they overlooked the healing.

After I read this verse, the Holy Spirit spoke to me. *What's your first response to your children? Do you look at your child as a whole or do you choose certain actions and behavior? Are you so consumed with training your child that you're not seeing their fruits of obedience?*

My friends, I encourage you to focus on the miracles, not the methods! Look at what God is doing, not on how it's done, when it's done, or the times it's simply not done. In regard to our children, we can laugh a little at the notion that sometimes their obedience feels like a miracle. Even when it's sporadic, go ahead and affirm your child!

We can stop at this parenting lesson, but let's dig deeper. What's so amazing about Jesus in this chapter is that He doesn't stop with the miracle, but continues with an Easter message. He could have left it as a lesson on the heart of Sabbath and healing, but He tells everyone, "My Father is always working, and so am I" (John 5:17 NLT). What is He working on? Establishing His Kingdom!

You see, the healing of this man wasn't merely a miracle. It was a foreshadowing: "the Father will show [Christ] how to do even greater works than healing this man. Then you will truly be astonished. For just as the Father gives life to those he raises from the dead, so the Son gives life to anyone he wants" (John 5:20-21 NLT).

Jesus then lays out the Gospel message: "I tell you the truth, those who listen to my message and believe in God who sent me have eternal life. They will never be condemned for their sins, but they have already passed from death into life" (John 5:24 NLT).

When it comes to salvation, there's no nitpicking. We don't have to be perfect; in fact, the Bible says we've *all* fallen short of the glory of God (Romans 3:23). Best of all, Jesus is not a dictator, but one who is full of grace and compassion (Psalm 145:8). We can rejoice that we follow a King who doesn't focus on methods, but brings miracles and the promise of eternal life.

Questions to Ponder

• Do you have a life situation where you feel immobile? Ask Jesus to give you His strength so that you may pick up your mat and walk.

Faith-Filled Ideas

Affirm, affirm, affirm! Choose to make today a day that you look at the positives in your children, your husband, and yourself!

• If your toddler wet her pants, don't get upset. (I still feel remorse—and this was nine years ago— so try to not follow my mistakes). Look at it as an opportunity to spend time together getting cleaned and changed.

• If your child helps you make dessert and the presentation leaves something to be desired, don't re-do it! Proudly show off her work to the family.

• If your child comes home with a poor grade on a test, affirm everything he did right!

journal

_____

_____

_____

_____

_____

_____

_____

journal

Walking with John

> ❝ Then Jesus declared, 'I am the bread of life. Whoever comes to me will never go hungry, and whoever believes in me will never be thirsty.' ❞
>
> ~ John 6:35

"Bread of Life? Jesus lived up to the title. But an unopened loaf does a person no good. Have you received the bread? Have you received God's forgiveness?"
~ Max Lucado

- Grab your Bible, journal and a snack—you'll need stamina for this chapter!
- Pray and ask the Holy Spirit to guide you through your study.
- Read John 6. Write John 6:35 in your journal and memorize it.

Now, you're ready to partake...

Jesus, the Bread of Life: Sustenance for the Spirit

By: Celi Turner

As mothers, we are often so preoccupied with nurturing others that we forget to feed ourselves. How many times have you reached the end of the day, lying in bed, and you feel your stomach rumbling, only to realize you've either forgotten to eat or have only picked at random samplings of mac & cheese or mushy melba toast? Nourishing ourselves is just as important as nourishing others; otherwise, we not only leave our bodies vulnerable to illness, but our spirits vulnerable to doubt and fear. Today's study will illustrate our need for spiritual food.

Today you are receiving instruction and sustenance directly from the source—Jesus, the Bread of Life. You read John chapter 6, a chapter in the Gospels that is packed with key events—miracles, even—plus some "hard teachings."

Let's begins today's nourishing meal with a recap of the events in John chapter 6:

1. Multitudes of people are following Jesus and His twelve disciples around to listen to His teachings, and—let's be honest—witness His miracles. Many are interested in Jesus merely as spectators at a sporting event who, once the spectacle is over, put away their fan gear and zeal until the next event.

2. Yet, Jesus is the perfect, patient *Rabbi* or teacher. Jesus understands that His followers and disciples have difficulty believing unless they see for themselves. So, Jesus sets up His lesson with a miracle: He bows his head to pray and give thanks, then turns an inadequate five loaves and two fish into baskets full enough to feed more than five thousand people! Jesus, in effect, gives them a very literal example of the "bread of life." Amazed by what they witness, the people start speculating about making Jesus king, but Jesus, knowing their intention is not the Father's will, withdrew to the mountain.

3. Later that evening, while the disciples were out on the water in a boat, Jesus actually *walks on water* to join them—but they freak out and don't recognize Him! Jesus has to reassure them that he is in fact Jesus by saying, "It is I; don't be afraid." Could it be that even Jesus' closest followers still foolishly fear the unknown and still doubt who Jesus is?

4. In the meantime, it doesn't take long for the crowds to realize Jesus, the headliner to their main event, has left. Without even giving themselves time to digest or understand the more obvious fish and loaves bread-of-life lesson, they get into boats to follow Jesus, and then they demand more signs of who Jesus is!

5. Jesus patiently attempts to make His bread of life lesson more clear. Jesus uses the example the people themselves brought up: The story of manna falling from heaven to feed God's people in the wilderness (Exodus 16). Jesus then further explains, "For the bread of God is the bread that comes down from heaven and gives life to the world"(John 6:32). But the people insist that Jesus give them *literal* bread of God! Then Jesus clearly states: "**I am the bread of life**" (John 6:35a).

6. How does the crowd respond? They start grumbling, doubting that Jesus, the son of Joseph the carpenter, could have come down from heaven. At this point, knowing that not everyone who hears will believe, Jesus reiterates, "I am the living bread that came down from heaven. Whoever eats this bread will live forever. This bread is my flesh, which I will give for the life of the world" (John 6:51). The story continues with the Jews starting to fight among themselves, taking literally what Jesus said about eating His flesh and drinking His blood! Some of them walk away from Jesus, saying, "This is a hard teaching" (John 6:60a).

Jesus' followers in John 6 clearly still don't understand the lesson. They continue to live in fear and doubt. They continue to believe only what they see and understand in the physical realm, while allowing their spiritual being to thirst and hunger from lack of sustenance.

Jesus was trying to teach them that they were not just flesh and blood, but spirit, and that the spirit also needs sustenance—bread of life— in the form of Jesus Himself. If even the people who walked and talked and ate with Jesus doubted, feared and failed to understand, how much more prone are we to miss the real miracle; that the bread of life, Jesus, is our primary sustenance.

So how do we receive sustenance from Jesus?

1. **To receive sustenance, we must first believe.** When fear and doubt creep in, I remind myself who Jesus is and declare it aloud.

   If you declare with your mouth, "Jesus is Lord," and believe in your heart that God raised him from the dead, you will be saved. (Romans 10:9)

   When Jesus spoke again to the people, he said, "I am the light of the world. Whoever follows me will never walk in darkness, but will have the light of life." (John 8:12)

2. **We receive sustenance through the Holy Spirit.** When I am overwhelmed with fear or doubt, it's usually because I have forgotten that I am not just flesh but also spirit. These verses remind me that the Holy Spirit guides and comforts me, Spirit to spirit.

   The Spirit gives life; the flesh counts for nothing. The words I have spoken to you— they are full of the Spirit and life. (John 6:63)

   And I will ask the Father, and he will give you another advocate to help you and be with you forever— the Spirit of truth. (John 14:16-17)

3. **We receive sustenance through God's Word.** If I don't take the time to read and reflect on God's Word each day, I become more ditzy (than usual), my mind spinning like a compass with no bearings. God's Word settles and focuses me on His promises.

   Jesus answered, "It is written: Man shall not live on bread alone, but on every word that comes from the mouth of God." (Matthew 4:4)

All Scripture is God-breathed and is useful for teaching, rebuking, correcting and training in righteousness, so that the servant of God may be thoroughly equipped for every good work. (2 Timothy 3:16-17)

4. We receive sustenance through prayer. Sometimes my prayers are bold and daring or sometimes mere whispers as disjointed as my thoughts, but I know Jesus hears each one when I pray expectantly.

And I will do whatever you ask in my name, so that the Father may be glorified in the Son. You may ask me for anything in my name, and I will do it. (John 14:13-14)

Rejoice always, pray continually, give thanks in all circumstances; for this is God's will for you in Christ Jesus. (1 Thessalonians 5:16-18)

When Jesus came as the Bread of Life, the earthly body broken on the altar of the cross as a sacrifice for our sins, He was not just guaranteeing us passage from this physical world into eternity; Jesus was also providing us with enough nourishment—basketsful—to counteract the inevitable doubt and fear of living on this side of heaven.

Dear mamas, just as you feed your body and your babies, you must also nourish your spirit in order to have enough spiritual food to sustain both you and your loved ones.

Feed yourselves to live and to give.

Walking with John

Questions to Ponder
• How are you doing at nurturing yourself in order to nurture your loved ones?

• What doubts or fears distract you from taking the time to nourish your spirit with the bread of life?

Faith-Filled Ideas
From the Questions to Ponder section above, write down one or two of those doubts or fears that distract you.

Next, write down a Scripture from this Bible study under each fear or doubt to help remind you to nourish yourself.

Lastly, pray aloud and/or write a prayer in your journal using the Scripture as a guide, and asking Jesus to help you with that distraction.

Example:

Fear: I am not competent enough to tackle all of my tasks.

"Rejoice always, pray continually, give thanks in all circumstances; for this is God's will for you in Christ Jesus" (1 Thessalonians 5:16-18).

Dear Jesus, help me to be joyful in all my tasks today; walk with me through them and give me strength and peace to finish them. I thank you for the gift of serving my family. Help me to focus on Your will today even in my busyness.

journal

_____

_____

Journal

Walking with John

Easter Garden

By: Tara Davis

Hi friends! I have a super fun Easter idea for you
to do with your kids this week. Make an Easter Garden!
This is a fantastic way to talk about each event of the Easter story.
My eight year old even drew and cut out a picture of Jesus and
used our little garden to reenact His glorious Resurrection.

WHAT YOU NEED:

- Terracotta saucer (the kind that goes under a planter, you can find one in a garden department)
- A small terracotta pot
- Soil
- Grass seed or wheat seed
- Twigs
- Twine (or hot glue gun)
- Small pebbles
- One larger rock

DIRECTIONS:

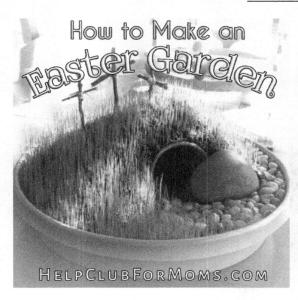

1. Lay the small pot on its side in the middle of the terracotta saucer.
2. Surround the pot with soil and cover with as much dirt as you would like to make a hill.
3. Sprinkle grass seed and cover with a thin layer of soil.
4. Lay pebbles in front of the opening of the pot to make a path and cover the entrance with a larger, flat stone to make a tomb.
5. Tie or glue twigs to make three crosses and insert on top of the hill.
6. Spray or sprinkle the soil with water daily and watch new life come to your garden.

This is the perfect time to start this activity if you want a nice, mature garden by Easter.

Use the garden to teach your children about Jesus' death and Resurrection. Your kids can make Jesus out of paper or a wooden peg to act out the story as you tell it or later in their play. This garden is both a beautiful Easter centerpiece and a story prop to connect your children to the events of Easter. *Make one today!*

Walking with John

~ Week Seven ~

Hello Friends,

It has been such a beautiful encouragement to venture through the book of John together! There is so much goodness and truth packed in these pages. We hope that Jesus has been speaking to you and we are praying for you!

As we ponder the idea of growing in Christ, recognize that Jesus provides the good soil in which to nurture our children. It's not all on us. We are sinners, frequently falling short of our Father's perfect parenting. We need grace upon grace! Am I right? Be encouraged that Jesus never, ever expects us to be perfect moms, not even close!

We mamas can be our own worst critics, focusing on what we aren't doing "right" for our kiddos instead of the good we accomplish. Dwelling on the negative causes much anxiety and stress. Rather, let's remember that all of our attempts at reaching our kids' hearts for the Lord or training their character are tiny seeds planted in fertile soil. We don't know when God will choose to water and grow our fruit, but we can feel confident that we have placed it in the hands of the perfect and most careful gardener. So mama, take some pressure off of yourself to perform. Your only job is to remain faithful and to trust! Jesus takes our seemingly small attempts (seeds) to nudge our kids in His direction, and turns them into a beautiful harvest we never even imagined!

Stay faithful in the small things, mama. You are doing great! Jesus loves those kids of yours more than you can ever know. Trust that what you are doing is enough and that God is smiling as He thinks of you!

In love,
Krystle Porter and the Help Club for Moms Team

If your children enter adulthood with a clear concept of who God is and what He wants them to do, you will have achieved the greatest accomplishment in life.
~ Dr. James Dobson

Mom Tips

By: Leslie Leonard

"Let your roots grow down into him, and let your lives be built on him. Then your faith will grow strong in the truth you were taught, and you will overflow with thankfulness." ~ Colossians 2:7 (NLT)

The Wise Woman Builds Her Spirit

- Unfollow (you don't have to unfriend) anybody on Facebook or Instagram that tempts you to feel envious, depressed, inadequate, or guilty. Perhaps you can fast from all social media this week.

- Take your quiet time outside this week. Grab your Bible, notebook, and coffee. Sit and listen to what God has to say to you. Be still in these moments and let the Holy Spirit work in your heart. Enjoy the beauty of your surroundings, and worship God for the beauty He has made.

The Wise Woman Loves Her Husband

- Call or text your husband a few times this week just to say "hello" and to see if there is anything you can do for him to ease the burden of his day. He will be glad to come home to a thoughtful wife.

- Give your husband a day off this weekend, no questions asked. Give him the chance to meet up with friends, go golfing, or just have a quiet moment to himself to clear his head. Do this with a cheerful heart, and listen to him when he gets home. Don't complain or act resentful; remember, this was a gift!

The Wise Woman Loves Her Children

- Children love it when we as moms take time out of our busyness to play with them! Devote at least 10 minutes per day this week to play with each of your children. Be silly and have fun! They may remember those 10 minutes for the rest of their lives!

- Hug your children and tell them you love them every day this week. In the hustle and bustle of life, it is easy to go all day without saying the most important words to your children.

The Wise Woman Cares For Her Home

- Clear all clutter from your kitchen table and counters this week. Put away all stray items that have landed in the kitchen. File paperwork and throw away any trash. Create a plan to avoid this situation in the future.

- Start a load of laundry first thing three days this week. When the wash cycle finishes, immediately move the load to the dryer. When the load finishes in the dryer, fold the clothes and immediately put them away. Do not let the clothes pile up on a couch or chair. Finish the task fully.

> Let anyone who is thirsty come to me and drink. Whoever believes in me,
> as Scripture has said, rivers of living water will flow from within them.
>
> ~ John 7:37-38

"Some journeys take us far from home. Some adventures lead us to our destiny."
  ~ C.S. Lewis

- Remember to call your prayer partner today! Keep it quick, and keep praying for each other throughout the week.

- Good Morning Precious One. Grab your favorite beverage, your Bible, your journal, and a pen. Join me as we soak in God's Word and read about a time when our Savior was not understood.

- Take a moment to read John 7.

He Was Not Understood

By: Pam Mays

For Easter, when I was in 3rd grade, my mom gave me this beautiful white, zippered King James Bible. I treasured this precious gift; I knew it was special. However, I did not understand what the Bible said. It wasn't that I couldn't read; I had not yet come to true faith in Christ. In a sense, I was like the Pharisees, not knowing or believing Jesus was God's Son, sent to be my Savior.

In John 7, leading up to Jesus' crucifixion, the Pharisees didn't believe Jesus was the Messiah. Thus, they refused to accept His teaching. They were content with their rituals, and their foolish hearts were closed to their long-awaited Messiah.

In John 7:28-32 we read:

> Then Jesus, still teaching in the temple courts, cried out, "Yes, you know me, and you know where I am from. I am not here on my own authority, but he who sent me is true. You do not know him, but I know him because I am from him and he sent me." At this they tried to seize him, but no one laid a hand on him, because his hour had not yet come. Still, many in the crowd believed in him. They said, "When the Messiah comes, will he perform more signs than this man?" The Pharisees heard the crowd whispering such things about him. Then the chief priests and the Pharisees sent temple guards to arrest him.

Do you understand who Jesus is today? Do you recall a time when you didn't understand God's Word?

Today, I love God and still treasure that little, white, zippered Bible my Mom gave me so long ago. I am thankful that Jesus became real in my life. I now understand the Word of God better as the Holy Spirit teaches me. I was fortunate to have an amazing, godly couple mentor me who read through Acts and Romans with me every Saturday morning for a year. They invited me to their church, where I met other believers who were welcoming and friendly. This gave me an amazing faith foundation when I was a "baby" Christian. They discipled me from God's Word and also through the incredible example of their lives. It was important to see what godliness looked like. They taught me that Easter is a precious time of remembering our Savior who came, died, and rose again to forgive you and me of our sins. Join me today in thanking God for loving us so much that He sent Jesus! "Thank You, Father God!"

Questions to Ponder

- Have you ever asked God to reveal Himself to you? If not, please talk to God about that now. Don't wait any longer!
- Do you feel far from God? Ask Him to expose any wrong attitudes, beliefs, and behaviors in your life. Repent (stop doing it), and ask God for forgiveness.

Faith-Filled Ideas

Continue reading God's Word, asking Him to give you wisdom and true understanding of what you are studying.

Find a sweet mama who is ahead of you or more seasoned in the Word to meet with at least once a month to discuss what you are reading.

If you don't have a Bible-believing church home, ask God to lead you to a fellowship where you can worship, serve, and learn together with other believers.

Walking with John

Journal

_____

_____

_____

_____

_____

_____

_____

_____

_____

_____

_____

_____

_____

_____

journal

_____

_____

_____

_____

_____

_____

_____

_____

_____

_____

_____

_____

_____

_____

_____

_____

_____

_____

_____

_____

_____

_____

_____

_____

_____

_____

_____

Walking with John

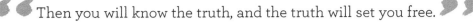

> ❝ Then you will know the truth, and the truth will set you free. ❞
>
> ~ John 8:32

"Where I found truth, there I found my God, who is the truth itself."
~ Augustine

- This is the day that the Lord has made, let us rejoice and be glad in it! I encourage you to have a quiet time with the Lord today. When you do, gather your Bible and journal, and sit at your Father's feet for a while.

- Please read John 8, and take note of John 8:31-36. These verses are Jesus' own words about our freedom in Him! Write verse 32 in your journal and pray about this freedom being continually revealed to you.

Jesus is Truth and He Brings Freedom

By: Rachel Jones

There is no one like Jesus. His name heals, brings freedom, forgives, loves, is patient, and is lasting. He is compassionate and full of grace, yet He is stern and challenges our faulty thinking and behavior. He is awe-inspiring and mysterious, yet He gladly reveals Himself to us when we seek Him. His Spirit pierces into the deepest part of our heart and soul, convicting us of sin. He is Truth, and His truth sets us free. He deserves our complete adoration and reverence!

There is a woman in the Bible who experienced all of Jesus first hand. She was spared her life and shown extreme compassion. She is referred to as the adulterous woman and her story is found in John 8. In verse 7, we find her caught in the act of adultery and on the edge of receiving horrible punishment from the Pharisees. However, Jesus steps in and takes the attention off of her and challenges everyone standing there, "If any one of you is without sin, let him be the first to throw a stone at her" (John 8:7).

Wow! I am so grateful for Jesus' compassion for that woman. No one dared throw a stone, and everyone eventually left.

> Jesus straightened up and asked her, "Woman, where are they? Has no one condemned you?" "No one, sir," she said. "Then neither do I condemn you," Jesus declared. "Go now and leave your life of sin." (John 8:10-11)

This woman could have been stoned to death, but Jesus wanted to redeem her from sin, not condemn her. There is no proof of course, but I would imagine the adulterous woman never returned to her former behavior, not because she feared dying, but because Jesus had liberated her with His forgiveness and love. It was her chance for a new beginning, a fresh start, freedom from her past!

These beautiful song lyrics from *Who Am I* by Casting Crowns perfectly express what I think she felt:

> Who am I, that the eyes that see my sin would look on me with love and watch me rise again?

And that is what Jesus does best. He sees us in our darkest moments and knows our evil thoughts. Nothing is hidden from His eyes. He yearns to see us rise again to make better decisions; decisions not based on fear, anxiety, and guilt, but on truth, love, and freedom.

But why is it so hard for us to live that way? Is it because we haven't accepted this truth for ourselves? As a young adult, I found it difficult to believe and obey God. My parents had such an amazing faith that I tended to lean on them. I grew up going to church, but I hadn't fallen in love with Jesus, nor experienced His transformative power for myself. We often act like the accusers in John 8:31-36; uncertain that we need a Savior, and resistant to changing our beliefs. We think we are "good" people who are better than others, giving us the right to judge while doing whatever we want.

However, Jesus speaks directly to this line of thinking: "I tell you the truth, everyone who sins is a slave to sin. Now a slave has no permanent place in the family, but a son belongs to it forever. So if the Son sets you free, you will be free indeed" (John 8:34-36).

That verse is your identity. You have been set free and adopted as a daughter of God! I pray that you begin to make the choice to be as gracious to others as Jesus was with you.

Questions to Ponder

• What are you thinking about right now? Journal about your thoughts. Quick! I know this is unorthodox, but God usually speaks to us when we spend time with Him, and then we forget it... or we don't take it seriously. But right now, write down what is on your heart and read it over every night this week. Pray about these thoughts and submit them to the Lord.

Faith-Filled Ideas

~*Who Am I*, by Casting Crowns

~*Who You Say I Am*, by Hillsong

These are two powerful songs that you will want to listen to, on repeat. Please listen to them while you have some quiet time. Try listening to worship music before bed. I turn the lights off and just listen with my eyes closed. It is so good for our minds to be reset at the end of the day so we are not awake all night with worry.

Journal

_____

_____

_____

_____

_____

_____

_____

_____

Journal

"Oh, without prayer what are the church's agencies, but the stretching out of a dead man's arm, or the lifting up of the lid of a blind man's eye? Only when the Holy Spirit comes is there any life and force and power."
~ Charles Spurgeon

- Dear, precious sister, reading the book of John has been so powerful, hasn't it? Today we are reading John 9 and focusing on the miracle-working power of Jesus! Find your special place where you meet with the Lord and read the entire ninth chapter of John and then read Acts 9:3-9 NIV and verse 17 in NKJV.

Opening Blind Eyes

By: Rae-Ellen Sanders

In John 9, we read about the blind man whom Jesus healed by making a concoction of mud and saliva and placing it on his eyes. Jesus then instructed him to wash. The man's obedience resulted in his sight: "So the man went and washed, and came home seeing" (John 9:7). This miracle is still being performed today in the lives of every believer.

Before we were saved by God's grace, we all had blind eyes. When we were lost to sin, or rather living in our former life, we could not fathom God's great love for us or understand His words to us in Scripture. A spiritual phenomenon had to happen: we first had to surrender to the need for a savior, seek forgiveness of sins, and ask to be made clean. It is at conversion that we encounter the living Christ, inviting Him into our lives and receiving His Spirit. This Holy Spirit, the third member of the triune God, is sent to live inside us and seals us as being born again into God's family.

Before this transformation, we aren't able to comprehend the mysteries of God. It is the same Jesus from John 9 who opens up our blind eyes to see Him and to see what He is doing. God's Word says when we seek Him, we will find Him (Jeremiah 29:13). As we actively grow as Christ followers and feed on Scripture, our eyes are opened to perceive the deep things of God. "Like newborn babies, crave pure spiritual milk, so that by it you may grow up in your salvation, now that you have tasted that the Lord is good" (1 Peter 2:2). "But solid food is for the [spiritually] mature, whose senses are trained by practice to distinguish between what is morally good and what is evil" (Hebrews 5:14 AMP). We must exercise our spiritual sight by walking in faith, studying the Bible, attending corporate worship services, and committing to a body of believers. These disciplines develop in us the ability to see God at work, to recognize His voice, and ultimately mature in our Christian walk.

Let's look at Acts 9 to learn about the life-changing conversion of the Apostle Paul, a committed persecutor of the first Christians. He was on a journey to Damascus to threaten, kill, and imprison followers of the Way:

> As he neared Damascus on his journey, suddenly a light from heaven flashed
> around him. He fell to the ground and heard a voice say to him, "Saul, Saul, why

are you persecuting Me?" "Who are you, Lord?" Saul asked. "I am Jesus, whom you are persecuting," he replied. "Now get up and go into the city, and you will be told what you must do." The men traveling with Saul stood there speechless; they heard the sound but did not see anyone. Saul got up from the ground, but when he opened his eyes he could see nothing. So they led him by the hand into Damascus. For three days he was blind, and did not eat or drink anything...Then Ananias went to the house and entered it. Placing his hands on Saul, he said, "Brother Saul, the Lord Jesus, who appeared to you on the road as you were coming here, has sent me so that you may see again and be filled with the Holy Spirit." Immediately, something like scales fell from Saul's eyes, and he could see again. He got up and was baptized. (Acts 9:1-9, 17-18 AMP).

Jesus has called us out of darkness into his marvelous light, and wants to give us eyes to *see Him*! Like Paul, listen to His voice and be transformed.

Questions to Ponder

• What consumes your daily vision? What we look at and spend our time on becomes our reality. The enemy wants us to be distracted by the things of this world. Take a minute to do an inventory. If you are convicted about not putting God first, commit to daily Bible reading, prayer, and meditation, singing hymns and praise songs, and choosing Christian reading material for yourself and your children.

• We can ask the Lord to heal our near-sightedness. If you know the Lord as your Savior but want to have the scales fall from your eyes, draw near to God, and He will draw near to you (James 4:8).

Faith-Filled Ideas

Don't lose sight of Jesus as you navigate this fallen world. Scripture reminds us that we are set apart: "But you are a chosen people, a royal priesthood, a holy nation, God's special possession, that you may declare the praises of him who called you out of darkness into his wonderful light" (1 Peter 2:9). It should be our joy to share Jesus with others and to tell them about what we see with our new eyes!

Pray for others to have a true glimpse of Jesus in you. Pray for your family members, friends, neighbors, and co-workers, that every blind eye will be opened and every hard heart softened.

journal

_____

_____

_____

_____

_____

_____

_____

_____

journal

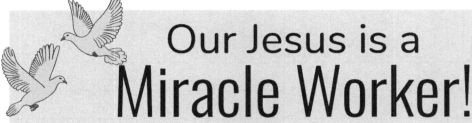

Our Jesus is a
Miracle Worker!

For Kids!

Lesson & Demonstration

As we consider all that Jesus has done for us as we anticipate Easter Sunday, it's great to teach our kids about how God is a miracle worker. He showed this to us through the Resurrection and so much more throughout Scripture!

To prepare for this lesson you will need:
1) Paper towels
2) Washable Markers

You can choose to do this activity by yourself with the kids, or as a family all together. The important thing, is that you are taking the intentional time to teach your kids about Jesus and show them how there is no one like our God!

This lesson is about how Jesus is a miracle worker!
Here is how you can begin this special time together:

Pray	Read	Listen
Take a moment to pray! Pray that God would help you to see through this fun activity, that He is a miracle worker!	Jeremiah 32:27 Luke 18:27 Mark 9:23 Matthew 17:20	"Waymaker" by Leeland "Miracles" by Jesus Culture

*** *Color Printable found at myhelpclubformoms.com* ***

Our Jesus is a
Miracle Worker!

Demonstration Guide

Miracle Art

Before you sit down to do this activity with your kids, grab your paper towels and markers. Draw a simple picture with the markers on on paper towel- a heart, rainbow, flowers, etc. Make sure that your design is full of color and your markers give it a deep coloring.

To show the miracle (demonstration):

1) Cover your art you made with overlapping paper towels like you see in photo number 1 (pictured above). You may want to make two so you can practice to make sure it works! Fill your sink with about an inch full of water, drop your "Miracle Art" in, and watch your design miraculously appear!

2) After you kids "ooh and ahh", let them make their own! Younger kids and older kids love this activity. Remind them as they color and create, that while this a fun project, Jesus really did perform real miracles,; feeding, healing and saving people! What an amazing God we serve!

*** *Color Printable found at myhelpclubformoms.com* ***

Are you looking for that perfect side dish to accompany your Easter dinner? Do you adore bacon? I have the perfect dish for you! My kids, hubby, and I are all huge fans of bacon. When added to just about any dish, it makes it better. Maybe that's an exaggeration, but the Carson family loves their bacon.

This green bean dish is not your grandma's green bean casserole. It's a little lighter, using fresh, nutritious, steamed green beans. Adding caramelized onions and the aforementioned bacon really takes it up a notch. Wow your guests this Easter or make this for your next family gathering.

DELECTABLE GREEN BEANS & BACON

By: Brandi Carson

Ingredients:

2 pounds fresh green beans, washed and ends cut off

1 pound bacon, chopped into medium-small pieces

1 large onion, cut in half and thinly sliced

2 cloves garlic, minced

Salt and pepper to taste

Directions:

1. After preparing your green beans, steam them in a steamer basket over boiling water for 5-7 minutes. You want them to look bright green and still have a bit of crunch left in them. Set aside.

2. In a large sauté pan, preheat to medium-high heat.

3. Cook bacon until crispy, 10-15 minutes. Remover with a slotted spoon. Remove bacon grease, leaving a few tablespoons in the pan for sautéing vegetables.

4. Lower heat to medium heat. Add garlic and sauté until aromatic, stirring continuously. Quickly add onions.

5. Sauté on medium to medium-low heat until caramelized. This process takes a while to make the onions nice and sweet, up to 20-25 minutes.

6. Once onions are caramelized, add steamed green beans and bacon, and season to taste with salt and pepper. Mix together and serve hot.

Walking with John

~ Week Eight ~

Dearest Mama,

There is so much assurance in John 10! Jesus our great Shepherd watches over, protects, and loves us so much that He calls us by name! Let that sink in for just a minute. He claims us as His own, and even surrendered His life so that we may share eternal life with Him:

> My sheep hear My voice, and I know them, and they follow Me. And I give them eternal life, and they shall never perish; neither shall anyone snatch them out of My hand. My Father, who has given them to Me, is greater than all; and no one is able to snatch them out of My Father's hand. I and My Father are one. (John 10:27-30)

How many of us can remember when our babies were newborn and our sweet bundles of joy would cry all the time? I specifically remember calling my mom who lived a country away from me at the time, perplexed with how to determine my baby's cry. How do you know if they are hungry, wet, or simply tired? Her response was that by spending time with my baby, I would learn his cues. Looking back, I realized it took time to determine each cry. As a seasoned mom, I could hear his cry from across a playground and know it was my child. Even now, with no more crying infants at home, I can still tell which of my children is walking in the room. Over time, we learn our children's noises. As His beloved sheep, we can become adept at deciphering God's voice and presence in our lives too.

As a shepherd knows each sheep, Jesus, the true Shepherd, knows us (John 10:3-6). He desires for us to be intimately acquainted with Him as Shepherd, Redeemer, Savior, and Friend. Then, we will hear His voice, cherish His presence, be assured of His leading, and live securely in His protection. I hope you take time to reflect on Jesus as your Shepherd this Lenten Season!

One of the flock,
Rae-Ellen Sanders and the Help Club for Moms Team

> *Our Good Shepherd has become the model for under-shepherds. His great concern is the good of the sheep. A good shepherd gives himself to the sheep. A thief comes to get something from the flock—wool or mutton. Jesus our Lord made every personal claim subservient to the blessing of his flock; even to giving His life that they might live.*
> ~ Walter J. Chantry

Mom Tips

By: Leslie Leonard

*"Let your roots grow down into him, and let your lives be built on him.
Then your faith will grow strong in the truth you were taught,
and you will overflow with thankfulness."* ~ Colossians 2:7 (NLT)

The Wise Woman Builds Her Spirit

- Listen to an audio Bible as you get ready every day this week.

- Read Ephesians 1. Rewrite it in your journal, inserting your name where applicable. It is a wonderful chapter of encouragement.

The Wise Woman Loves Her Husband

- Write a couple of short notes to your husband this week, telling him things you love or appreciate about him! Put them in unexpected places like his lunch, the dashboard of his car, his sock drawer, etc.

- Encourage your children to write or draw about all the things they love about their dad, why they love spending time together, and how he makes them happy. Hide their notes in your husband's work bag, or tuck them in his gym clothes. Consider framing them for his desk at work to encourage him over and over again.

The Wise Woman Loves Her Children

- Read a favorite chapter book from your childhood to your kids at bedtime. You will enjoy reading it to your children, and the joy of reading is contagious. You will all find yourselves looking forward to bedtime this week!

- Dye Easter eggs with your children. Boil the eggs in advance. Wear old clothes and prepare for a messy and fun afternoon. Don't forget to take some pictures, including some of mom laughing in the chaos! Everyone can work together to clean up.

The Wise Woman Cares For Her Home

- Meal plan based on what you currently have in your pantry and freezer. Be creative and resourceful. Use up the dry goods and items you have on hand instead of spending money at the grocery store. Play a game with yourself and see how many meals you can make with the items you have on hand.

- Choose one day this week to clean under the sink in your bathrooms. Remove everything and wipe down the entire area. Throw away any expired cosmetics or bath products. Remove items that do not belong in the bathroom and put them in the proper room. Replace all items in an organized manner.

> The thief comes only in order to steal and kill and destroy.
> I came that they may have and enjoy life,
> and have it in abundance [to the full, till it overflows].
> ~ John 10:10 (AMP)

"The devil steals from people in such a deceptive way that he often accomplishes his evil goal before they even know he has stolen from them!"
~ Rick Renner

- It's time to pray with your prayer partner! Remember, prayer moves mountains!

- Stop and pray before you read today's study, asking God to clothe you with Christ's armor. Did you know that Christ's armor helps you successfully resist the attacks of the enemy?

- Then, ask God to speak to you through this study. Jeremiah 29:13 promises that we will find God when we seek Him with *all* our heart! Quiet yourself and seek Him with your whole heart.

The Enemy Within

By: Kristi Valentine

Steal. Kill. Destroy. Jesus speaks these words of war in John 10:10. 1 Peter 5:8 says it again: "Stay alert! Watch out for your great enemy, the devil, who prowls around like a roaring lion looking for someone to devour."

Ironically, we're hardly aware enough to fight it. The robbery can be physical, emotional, mental, or spiritual. And although nothing may be literally stolen from you, I challenge you today to dig deeper with me into your thoughts and feelings. Insidiously, our enemy works to destroy, steal from, and kill us through our thought lives. Take the time to stop and do some extra examination!

Smoothly and seamlessly, the devil tricks us by planting worldly, negative, harmful ideas in our minds: "This is too hard; I can't do it anymore." "These kids are driving me crazy." "I'm bored." We blindly receive these unbiblical ideas as "normal." After all, they match with most other moms' thoughts. But did you know that those sweet mamas are under attack too? We shouldn't be comparing ourselves with the people around us. Instead, we should be asking ourselves, "Do my thoughts and feelings line up with Scripture?"

As a mom, when you feel anxious and overwhelmed, is it easy to stop, gently look into your children's eyes, and smile at them? No! Your sweet children feel like a frustrating distraction, right? And as a wife, when you feel irritable because of the things your husband does wrong, are you able to lovingly, joyfully go the extra mile to make your marriage thrive? Absolutely not! You feel mistreated! Your feelings are surely under attack.

As a mom and a wife, God's calling is for you to love your family well, with soft eyes, kind words, and servant leadership. On the other hand, the devil is doing everything he can to keep you from fulfilling that. The battle is real!

Sweet mama, what feelings need to be in your heart in order to respond more gently to your children? How can you adjust the voice in your mind to appreciate and invest in your husband? Ultimately, what can you do to fight for your family?

Every morning when you wake up, quietly pray out loud for yourself and every person in your family, resisting the devil for them in Jesus' name and placing each piece of Christ's armor on them, especially the shield of faith, which extinguishes all of the flaming arrows of the enemy.

This battle plan is directly from God's Word. James 4:7 says, "Resist the devil, and he will flee from you." Philippians 2:9 says that the name of Jesus is above every name. And finally, Paul says in Ephesians 6:10-17, immediately after talking about family relationships, that we are to clothe ourselves in the full armor of Jesus Christ every day. Wearing the armor, we'll be able to stand firm, resist the devil, and be victorious against all his attacks.

Friend, your family is a battlefield, and if you are not aware of it, then you can't even fight. Be alert. Arm yourself. And be encouraged that you are able to win the battle against the enemy!

Walking with John

Questions to Ponder

• What can I do to be more aware of my thoughts and feelings? On what truth can I meditate to transform my thoughts to godly ones?

• Are there times when I'm more vulnerable to worldly, negative, harmful thoughts and feelings? Are there books, shows, websites, or situations that tempt me to believe the lies of the enemy?

Faith-Filled Ideas

Invite a friend to be an accountability partner you can call when tempted to believe thoughts and feelings that might not be true. This is someone who will test your ideas, pray with you, and lead you toward the right path.

Renew your mind! Ephesians 4:23 says to let the Holy Spirit make your mind new. Romans 12:2 (NLT) says, "Don't copy the behavior and customs of this world, but let God transform you into a new person by changing the way you think." What is one worldly belief or habit you want to release so the Holy Spirit can renew your mind?

journal

_____

_____

_____

_____

_____

_____

_____

_____

journal

_____
_____
_____
_____
_____
_____
_____
_____
_____
_____
_____
_____
_____
_____
_____
_____
_____
_____
_____
_____
_____
_____
_____
_____
_____
_____
_____
_____
_____

Walking with John

Lent ~ Week Eight ~ Day Ten

> ❝ This illness…is for the glory of God,
> so that the Son of God may be glorified through it. ❞
> ~ John 11:4 (ESV)

"Take my struggles and use them for your glory. But whatever you do, please don't leave me the same."
~ Joanna Weaver

- Take some time to read through John 11, John 12:1-8, and Luke 10:38-42. Ask the Lord what He would like for you to learn from Him today as you look at the lives of Mary and Martha.

Humbly Trust In Jesus

By: Carmen Brown

I have learned a lot from Mary and Martha over the years. Observing their brief interactions with Jesus can teach us a lot about their relationships with Him. You may know them best from Luke 10:38-42, where we see them at a dinner where Jesus is the guest of honor. In this glimpse of them, we learn from Jesus that Mary had chosen the most important thing—Jesus Himself—and that Martha was anxious about many things. Today, we will focus on John 11 as they grieved for their brother, Lazarus, who had recently died. What lesson can we learn as we observe them in their grief?

Verse five in John 11 says, "Jesus loved Martha and her sister and Lazarus." Interestingly, in the next verse, it says, "because He loved them, when He heard that Lazarus was ill, He stayed two days longer in the place where He was" (John 11:6 ESV). If Jesus loved them, why didn't He go to them right away?

Do you ever feel that if Jesus loved you, He would answer your prayers right away and never leave you or a loved one waiting in a place of sadness or sickness or even close to death? That seems to go against how we view love from God, and yet it very clearly states that *because* He loved them, He waited. Jesus also said in verse four that, "This illness does not lead to death. It is for the glory of God so that the Son of God may be glorified through it." Can you look back on a time in your life when you felt like God was taking too long to answer a prayer, but then when it was answered, you could see how the time spent waiting for that answer gave God all of the glory? Or, you may be in a time now, waiting for an answered prayer. You may have been praying for many years for a restored marriage, a wayward child, or healing of a lengthy illness. I hope you see in these verses that sometimes the purpose of God's answer of "wait" is to show you His great love for you and to strengthen your faith! In verse 14, Jesus said, "Lazarus has died, and for your sake I am glad that I was not there, so that you may believe." Jesus was prepared to teach those mourning for Lazarus and His disciples something powerful in allowing Lazarus to die.

Continuing in her grief, in verse 20, Martha went and met Jesus before He was even in their village. Mary stayed inside grieving with the many friends who had come to console them. Martha says, "Lord, if you had been here, my brother would not have died. But even now I know that whatever you ask from God, God will give you." A little while later we see in verse 32 Mary says the same thing: "Lord, if you had been there, my brother would not have died." They say the same thing to

Walking with John

Jesus, but the difference is in the way Jesus responds to each one. To Martha, Jesus gives a strong reminder of who He is and what He can do. With Mary, "...he was deeply moved in his spirit and greatly troubled" and then, He wept (John 11:33, 35 ESV). Martha began questioning Jesus again in verse 38 before Jesus performed His miracle. When Jesus told them to remove the stone, she says,

> "Lord, by this time there will be an odor for he has been dead four days." And Jesus said, "Did I not tell you that if you believed you would see the glory of God?" (John 11:39-40)

The glory of God was certainly revealed when Lazarus came out of the tomb alive! Can you imagine? Praise the Lord who overcame death!

We observe both women getting valuable insight from Jesus, but even in that, we see one who trusted Jesus and His ways without question. What can we learn from these differing attitudes? Martha was walking with Jesus and believing, but everything was a struggle with her because she couldn't rest in Jesus and trust Him. Mary still had the same struggles and deep grief. But in that grief, she took a posture of humility before Him, falling at His feet and stating that she knew what He could do without questioning why He didn't do it. He loved and cared for both women, but one was always putting up a fight and one lived in humble trust.

My prayer for you is that you learn to live in humble trust as Mary did. Put down your work, and lay your grief humbly at His feet. Trust that He sees you, knows you, and loves you! Wait and see what He will do!

Questions to Ponder

• Which sister do you see in yourself? Are you in a place of questioning why something in your life is going the way it is? Are you the first to run to Jesus to "tell Him what's what" or do you humbly approach Him, drawing closer to Him through each struggle?

Faith-Filled Ideas

Ask the Lord to help you to trust that He cares for you and will work everything for His glory. Lay your burdens down at His feet knowing that His yoke is easy and His burden is light (Matthew 11:28-30).

journal

_____

_____

_____

_____

_____

_____

_____

_____

journal

Walking with John

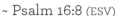 I have set the Lord always before me;
Because He is at my right hand I shall not be moved.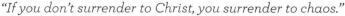

~ Psalm 16:8 (ESV)

Walking with John

"If you don't surrender to Christ, you surrender to chaos."
  ~ E. Stanley Jones

- Spend an extra 10 minutes in your quiet time today reading the entire 12th chapter of John.

- Pray and ask God what He wants you to learn today. Open your heart and mind to what today's study has to offer.

Set Your House in Order

By: Leslie Leonard

I can imagine the scene when Jesus arrived in Jerusalem. I wish I was sitting on one of the city walls watching the scene from above, taking in the hustle and bustle of the day: people gathering in the streets, waving palm branches, and shouting "Hosanna! Blessed is He who comes in the name of the Lord!" as Jesus rides by on a donkey (John 12:13). What a day for celebration!

Although this time seemed celebratory, Jesus immediately sat with his disciples and others to teach. He was getting His house in order before His departure. Starting in Chapter 12, verse 35 (ESV), we read:

> Then Jesus said to them, "A little while longer the light is with you. Walk while you have the light, lest darkness overtake you; he who walks in darkness does not know where he is going. While you have the light, believe in the light that you may become sons of light." These things Jesus spoke, and departed, and was hidden from them.

These are the last words of Jesus' public ministry. He refers to Himself as the light. Like a candle or flashlight gives light in a darkened room, Jesus Christ gives us a lighted path in our lives, and we are to walk with Him in confidence. Without Him, our vision is dim, our path unclear. We are also told to believe in the light. If we maintain hope and faith, we can continually hone our character to become more Christlike.

If we as believers do not have our spiritual house in order, we live a life in chaos. We allow the world to rule our lives instead of God. A simple rule to follow is **God–Husband–Children–Job–Everything Else.** Until you choose to put God first, you will never feel at ease or at peace in your life. While faith is a gift from God, we are commanded to be watchful and stand firm in the faith (1 Corinthians 16:13). We are to nurture our relationship with God by seeking Him. The Scripture, the Holy Spirit, the Gospel, creation itself—all reveal God's character, heart, and plan. Follow the light He has provided, and become "sons of light." Here are some great ways to strengthen your faith:

- **Pray every day.** This does not have to be a very long prayer. Just take a few minutes and thank God for all He has done for you and turn over any issues you might be facing in your life. James 5:16 tells us "The prayer of a righteous man is powerful and effective."

- **Establish a regular quiet time.** Read the Bible, meditate, and look for ways to apply what you have learned. If you have small children, maybe set your alarm an hour earlier so you can have that time alone before they get up for the day. Make the sacrifice. When we seek God first, we will be blessed (Matthew 6:33). Psalm 46:10 tells us, "Be still, and know that I am God. I will be exalted among the nations, I will be exalted in the earth!"

- **Attend a small group or Sunday school class.** We are called to fellowship with other believers, and a small group in your church is a great start. If you currently are not attending church, make a list of a few you have been meaning to check out and go this Sunday. Matthew 18:20 (ESV) tells us "For where two or three are gathered in my name, there am I among them"

- **Memorize Scripture.** Commit to memorizing one new verse each week. 2 Timothy 3:16 (ESV) tells us "All Scripture is breathed out by God and profitable for teaching, for reproof, for correction, and for training in righteousness."

By taking the time to build your biblical foundation, you will become more spiritually sound. I know your relationship with the Lord will grow deeper and your life will be blessed.

Will you join me in choosing to set our spiritual houses in order?

Questions to Ponder

• Do you take time to talk to God? It's easy and is just like talking to your best friend, except that He loves you more than anyone else on the face of the earth! God always has time for you and never tires of hearing your voice.

Faith-Filled Ideas

Pray aloud with your husband every night this week. Take turns praying blessings over your home and family. Lift up your concerns and burdens, and turn them over to the Lord. Be vulnerable in front of your spouse and the Lord. Praying together can be intimate and bring you closer as a couple, if you allow yourselves to be vulnerable. Praying aloud is an intimate act; it allows you to be vulnerable in front of other people. Allow that vulnerability to bring you closer as a couple.

Set up a quiet time basket. Gather your notebooks, devotion books, Bibles, favorite pens, and notecards. Keep them together in a portable basket, something with handles. This way you can have your quiet time anywhere, anytime. As moms, we have to be flexible and prepared when a quiet moment happens. My moments often come when my girls are playing outside. I can grab my basket, sit on the patio table, and spend some time with Jesus.

journal

_____

_____

_____

_____

_____

journal

Walking with John

HOMEMADE
Resurrection Eggs

By: Tara Davis

Hi friends! As Easter is drawing closer, I have been preparing
activities to share with my kids that will teach them more about our Savior.
I have an easy one that I want to share with you. If you have always wanted to do Resurrection Eggs
with your kids, but have never gotten around to purchasing them, here is a fun, inexpensive
alternative! *Bonus*: You should be able to use items you already have around your house.

WHAT YOU NEED: 12 plastic Easter eggs

DIRECTIONS:

1. Number each egg on the outside with stickers or a permanent marker.

2. Fill each egg using what you can find around the house (and printing or drawing little pictures for those items you can't find). For instance, nickels or dimes work for the silver coins, a bit of stem from a rose bush or thorny weed easily represents the thorns, sticks tied together with string can symbolize the cross, and a little paper sign can stand in for the "King of the Jews" plaque. Simple as can be!

Egg 1: Cracker or bread – Matthew 26:26

Egg 2: Silver Coins – Matthew 26:14-16

Egg 3: Purple Cloth – Matthew 27:28

Egg 4: Thorns – Matthew 27:29

Egg 5: Rope – Mark 15:15

Egg 6: Cross – John 19:16-17

Egg 7: Nail – John 19:18

Egg 8: Sign that says, "This is the king of the Jews." – Luke 23:38

Egg 9: Sponge (with vinegar on hand to let kids smell) – Matthew 27:48

Egg 10: Cloves or Spices – Luke 23:5-6

Egg 11: Rock – Matthew 27:59-60

Egg 12: Empty! – Matthew 28:55-56

3. You can jot each Scripture on a slip of paper and place in the corresponding egg. Or you can use this fantastic free printable to have the verses at your fingertips each day. http://bit.ly/2n2fPqq

4. Another option is to read the book *Benjamin's Box* to explain the concept of the resurrection eggs. We have it in our library system, and I bet you do too!

I'm so excited to use these eggs this year! I love finding sweet, hands-on ways to teach my kids about the life and love of Jesus. Would you join me?

Walking with John

~ Week Nine ~

Dear Precious One of the Most High,

What a journey this has been, walking together through the chapters of the Gospel of John. It touches me at my core to open the book of John and see all the red-lettered words of Jesus; it's personal, Jesus speaking to you and me.

We are five weeks into the Lenten season and our study continues to deepen through the truth of the Gospel. How are you growing in this study? Aren't you thankful, as I am, that Help Club has directed our focus on the Lenten season? If recognizing Lent has not been a part of your tradition in the past, you are not the only one; it is new for me, too! Did you know that Lent is one of the oldest observations in the Christian calendar? It is 40 days of "a time set aside" for self-examination and penitence. Some choose to deny themselves by fasting from a specific food (chocolate), a pleasure (TV), or a habit (using electronics). Others practice a discipline like prayer, service, or forgiveness.

However you choose to observe Lent, as you examine yourself, remember today, tomorrow, and in all your days to come, you are precious to God. He has sealed His love for you with His Holy Spirit, alive in you as your guide and advocate, always! In the remaining days of Lent, seek Him, know Him deeper, and grow in Him. Allow Him to come into every part of your life; surrender, hands wide open. Fully embrace the depth of His love for you. He loved you so much that He died for you! Why not remain in Him? We can do nothing apart from Him, and why would we want to? Jesus calls you His friend. He chose *you*. He paid it *all*. He gave all for you, sweet child of God! Take His hand, let Him lead you.

Blessings as you surrender,
Melissa Lain and the Help Club for Moms Team

Let's walk with Him. Let's see how Jesus spent His final days.
Enter the holy week and observe. Feel His passion. Sense His power.
Hear His promise that death has no power. Let's follow Jesus on his final journey.
For by observing His, we may learn how to make ours.

~ Max Lucado, On Calvary's Hill

Mom Tips

By: Leslie Leonard

"Let your roots grow down into him, and let your lives be built on him. Then your faith will grow strong in the truth you were taught, and you will overflow with thankfulness." ~ Colossians 2:7 (NLT)

The Wise Woman Builds Her Spirit

• Pray about the atmosphere you want for your home. Do you want it to be fun, cozy, open and inviting, tidy, peaceful, etc.? You do you, and create a unique haven to fit your special family.

• Take yourself out on a date this week. Choose something you love to do but rarely have time for. You could browse the stacks at the local library, go for a hike, people-watch at your favorite coffee shop, or take an adult education class.

The Wise Woman Loves Her Husband

• Find ways to make your husband smile this week—bonus points for getting him to laugh! Notice the quirky things your kids do and say, and laugh with your husband as you recount their antics.

• Plan a date night with your husband; something new to keep things exciting. Make all the arrangements, including finding a babysitter, making reservations, or paying in advance, if possible. Or, have a "date night in." Put the children to bed and make a fancy dinner for two. Dress up, set the table with real plates, and light some candles.

The Wise Woman Loves Her Children

• Make Easter sugar cookies with children this week. Let them help roll out the dough, cut out the shapes, and decorate once cooked. Remember, it will be messy, so plan ahead and don't stress. It will be fun. Make extras and take them to your neighbors or your pastoral staff.

• Take your children on a "date" this week. You might need to spread this out over several weeks, depending on how many children you have. Let each child select a reasonable activity for you to spend some one-on-one time. Let the child talk to you about whatever is on his or her heart. Remember to listen. End your time with a special prayer.

The Wise Woman Cares For Her Home

• Pray over the rooms of your home. Walk from room to room and ask God to bring peace, joy, and happiness to all who walk the floors of your home. In the rooms of your children, ask God to be present always in their lives and that they will seek Him first and always.

• Teach your children a new household task. Even small children can learn simple tasks like sweeping or folding laundry. Older children can tackle the dishes or cleaning bathrooms. You know what your children can handle.

"Does God ask us to do what is beneath us? This question will never trouble us again if we consider the Lord of heaven taking a towel and washing feet."
~ Elisabeth Elliot

- Have you made your weekly prayer call? Habitually discussing God and praying with a friend is a great way not only to hear His voice but also to confirm that it is His voice you're hearing.

- Dear Sister in Christ, as we embark on this time of reflection of what Christ did for us on the cross, let us look at the Last Supper and what Jesus was telling us when he washed his disciples' feet. Open your Bible and turn to John 13:1-35.

Walking with John

Clean Your House!

By: Rae-Ellen Sanders

My husband and I have been studying our Hebraic roots and even hosted Passover this year. I loved learning all about the symbolism of the ceremonial Seder dinner! One of the things that really struck me was the washing of hands and feet during the celebration. We read in John 13:3-17 that Jesus washed His disciples' feet as well. What is so interesting is that the Jews wash to be cleansed of sin in order to partake in the meal. Jesus washes the disciples' feet not only as a ritual, but also as an example of how we are to love one another! We are going to take a deeper look into John 13, but first a little history on Passover.

The Lord's Passover is also known as the Day of Preparation for the Feast of Unleavened Bread, which is usually the seven days preceding the Resurrection (Luke 22:1). At the start of Passover, the first day of unleavened bread, Jewish people remove all the leaven from their homes (Exodus 12:15,19-20). A search is conducted with a candle to check all the nooks and crannies where leaven might exist. When Peter and John went to make arrangements to secure a place for the Passover meal, they would have removed all the leaven from the upper room (Luke 22:7-13).

Leaven's definition is yeast that is added to bread to make it rise. Its action is to ferment or permeate and ultimately modify. In the Bible, it represents sin and is removed from the house so that one could come before the Lord without sin. "Wash yourselves, make yourselves clean; remove the evil of your deeds from My sight" (Isaiah 1:16 NASB). Purification has always been required before coming into the presence of the Lord. The Old Testament is full of instructions for the priests to ceremonially wash themselves before entering the inner court, known as the Holy of Holies, to commune with God. In fact, Moses had to take off his sandals to be in the Lord's presence (Exodus 3:5).

As we all know, sin has the capacity to do the same thing in our lives. Left unrepented, it spreads and grows. We too need to clean our "houses" and come before the Lord with a pure heart. I love this revelation and how it applies to us as Christians. We need to search our hearts during this season, and ask the Lord to cleanse us of any unrighteousness as we focus on Christ's sacrificial death, resurrection, and ascension.

At the Last Supper, Jesus completes this task prior to the meal by spiritually searching the hearts of his disciples. He finds leaven (the representation of corruption or sin) in Judas. Knowing Judas would betray Him, Jesus hands him the piece of bread and commands him to go, purging the leaven from the house and therefore removing sin from the presence of God (John 13:26-27).

As part of the Passover celebration, participants wash their hands and feet before eating. This act of preparation symbolizes removing their evil deeds. When you tell your kids to wash their hands before eating dinner, your desire is to keep them from ingesting dirt and getting sick. In the same way, God is telling us to remove sin from our lives too! Christ shows us, through the example of washing the disciples' feet, how to serve each other and to bear each other's burdens. Jesus tells them, "If I don't wash your feet, you have no part with me" (John 13:8). What He is saying is that you can't walk with Him in ministry and be effective if you don't let Him wash you. When Peter heard that, he enthusiastically requested that Jesus wash not only his feet, but his hands and head as well! Jesus simply responds, "Those who have had a bath need only to wash their feet; their whole body is clean" (John 13:10). Once we have accepted Jesus as our Lord and Savior, we are "bathed" all over and cleansed by His blood, once and for all (Hebrews 10:14).

Questions to Ponder

- Jesus exhorts us: "For I have given you an example, that you should do as I have done to you. Most assuredly, I say to you, a servant is not greater than his master; nor is he who is sent greater than he who sent him" (John 13:15-16 NKJV). How can we "wash each other's feet?" Colossians 3:16 (NKJV) says, "Let the word of Christ dwell in you richly in all wisdom, teaching and admonishing one another in psalms and hymns and spiritual songs, singing with grace in your hearts to the Lord."

Faith-Filled Ideas

Washing someone's feet might mean taking action and helping in another's circumstances. Humbling ourselves in service blesses the person being helped, as well as ourselves. It is yet another way we are molded into His image. As mamas, we *need* community with other sisters in the Lord. Creating relationships requires us to get involved; we can't remain detached. God doesn't want us to just "feel" sympathy for others, but to exert a willingness to respond. He just might want us to weep with those who weep, or help another mom who needs a break. "Well meaning" is powerless when comforting others. God often extends healing through the compassion of His people. As the body of Christ, we are called to bear each other's burdens (Galatians 6:2). Ask the Lord to show you who you can love today!

journal

_____

_____

_____

_____

journal

Lent ~ Week Nine ~ Day 13

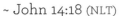

> No, I will not abandon you as orphans—I will come to you.
> ~ John 14:18 (NLT)

Walking with John

"I am leaving you with a gift—peace of mind and heart. And the peace I give is a gift the world cannot give. So don't be troubled or afraid."
~ Jesus, John 14:27 (NLT)

- Dear Mom, it's so easy to become anxious when a trial arises in our lives. Often, we feel worried because our situation seems hopeless. However, Jesus told us not to let our hearts be troubled or afraid. In today's devotional, we will learn why we don't have to feel distressed or unsettled. God had a plan to send The Holy Spirit, our Advocate, Comforter, and Helper to live inside of us! He offers us peace of mind and heart, instead of unrest and worry.

- Read John chapter 14. As you read and study this chapter, seek to know your Father, not just knowledge about Him. His Holy Spirit is a personal gift, given to empower you with everything you need for a godly life. If you believe in Jesus, He lives in you and desires to fill you until you are overflowing!

Don't Be Troubled or Afraid

By: Mari Jo Mast

It takes faith to believe God is with you when hard times hit. I'll never forget the night our little grandson's blood sugar spiked so high that it wouldn't register on the blood glucose monitor. He was one year old. I felt angry at the enemy and betrayed by God. How could this happen when the Word says, "God is love" (1 John 4:8b)? I felt isolated and alone, like He didn't care or hear my prayers.

In the beginning of that trial, I completely forgot about the Holy Spirit's presence in my life. The enemy wanted me to feel hopeless, and I went to bed completely devastated. My husband and I were already standing in faith for divine healing with another member of our family. Satan wanted us to think we had zero power, and to give up all hope.

I will always remember how the Holy Spirit spoke to me that night as I lay in a fetal position, wallowing in fear and despair. What He declared broke my fear into a thousand pieces and delivered peace inside of me instead! The Spirit of Jesus was with me. I was not abandoned, even though I didn't feel Him and even though I had forgotten He was with me. He was there all along.

With a distinct and clear message! He spoke truth (it echoed on and on and on). Jesus declared that my Grandson was and is a healthy baby. Even though what I saw in the physical realm was very different from what He was decreeing, I agreed with His proclamation. I know God speaks truth, and it's my job to agree by faith, declaring with Him and believing, regardless of what my eyes tell me.

Dear sister, when the enemy comes against us full force, we can know God still is *for us*, no matter what (Romans 8:31-39)! When we feel abandoned and alone, it is not true. Jesus is with us all of the time. He gives us everything we need in order to overcome, through the person of the Holy Spirit! Even when we forget, He is with us and helps us! We have this hope because God never fails in keeping His promises.

But when the Father sends the Advocate as my representative—that is, the Holy Spirit,—He will teach you everything and will remind you of everything I have told you. I am leaving you with a gift—peace of mind and heart. And the peace I give is a gift the world cannot give. So don't be troubled or afraid. Remember what I told you: I am going away, but I will come back to you again. (John 14:26-29 NLT)

My friend, John 14 assures us Jesus' Spirit resides in us; we don't need to fear. He died so we could have a relationship with our beautiful Heavenly Father through His Spirit. He dearly loves us, and wants to bring freedom into *every* area of our lives.

Do you believe in Jesus? The gift of the Holy Spirit (our Comforter, Helper, and Advocate) comes through believing and surrendering—putting our hope in His finished work on the cross. Can you trust in His inherent goodness, even when you feel hopeless?

As a believer, you hold inside of you the most treasured gift in the whole wide world. You have what the world could never give you—peace of heart and mind. Continue to ask The Holy Spirit to fill you to overflowing.

If you want to believe, repent of your sins and ask Jesus to come live inside of you. Receive the promise of His indwelling Spirit by faith. This is where your victory lies—freedom from anxiety, worry, and fear.

Jesus never leaves those who put their trust in Him! No matter what you're facing, read God's Word and listen to His Spirit who teaches you all things. And pray. Talk to God about absolutely everything. He genuinely cares about the trials you face. Your relationship with Him will steadily grow deeper and more vibrant.

Something to always remember: God speaks truth—it's your job to believe and agree with what He says, regardless of your circumstances. He cannot lie (Hebrews 6:18).

One word from the Holy Spirit who dwells in you has the power to obliterate (utterly wipe out) your greatest fear. He is with you *all* of the time; only believe.

Questions to Ponder

• What hard things are you currently facing? Remember God is gracious. Even when you forget He's with you, He's there! He never leaves.

• Ask Him for His counsel, direction, and help.

Faith-Filled Ideas

Memorize John 14:27. When you're hit with hard times, refer to this verse. It will encourage you to remember that the Spirit of Jesus lives inside of you and is your Helper at *all* times.

> I am leaving you with a gift. Peace of mind and heart. And the peace I give is a gift the world cannot give. So don't be troubled or afraid. (John 14:27 NLT)

journal

_____

_____

Walking with John

journal

_____
_____
_____
_____
_____
_____
_____
_____
_____
_____
_____
_____
_____
_____
_____
_____
_____
_____
_____
_____
_____
_____
_____
_____
_____
_____
_____
_____
_____

Walking with John

> **❝** I am the vine; you are the branches. If you remain in me and I in you, you will bear much fruit; apart from me you can do nothing. **❞**
> ~ John 15:5

"However strong the branch becomes, however far away it reaches...all its beauty and all its fruitfulness ever depend upon that one point of contact where it grows out of the vine. So be it with us too."
  ~ Andrew Murray

- Are you feeling tired today? I believe God has refreshment for each of us, as we look at John 15.
- Take a few minutes to read John 15, then write verse five in your journal.

Filling Your Tank

By: Kari Trent Stageberg

Have you ever been going through life thinking everything is great when you suddenly realize there is a *big* problem? Ladies, I recently had that exact experience.

My husband Joey and I were getting ready to order takeout for the 3rd night in a row. We had been too busy to get groceries, and honestly, an empty fridge was becoming the norm at our house.

I was about to place the order, when Joey asked, "Kari, how did we get so busy that we don't even have food in our fridge?"

I was surprised by his question, and honestly, I didn't have an answer.

He continued, "I feel so drained. Don't you feel empty? Like we are just going through the motions and missing important things that make our lives joyful and *healthy*?"

I was stunned. But as I processed his question, I realized he was right.

It had been a busy season. While we made our marriage a priority, we failed to make things like time with Jesus, friends, or even healthy eating a priority. I had assumed things would slow down. But months had gone by, and it was just getting more hectic. This had left Joey and me feeling frustrated, and at the end of our ropes most days—not the best way to spend life as newlyweds.

While I thought about Joey's question, the Lord gave me a "picture" to help me understand what was happening. I'd love to share it with you.

In the "picture," I had just been given my dream car. I was so excited that I drove that car *everywhere*. I watched as the gas gage on the car indicated the fuel level was getting lower and lower. But every time I passed a gas station, I decided I could go a little bit further without filling up. After all, I didn't want to be late for my next adventure.

However, a few weeks later, while I was driving, the car began to make a sickening clunking noise and slowly chugged its way to a stop. I had run out of gas.

A man stopped to help me, but he only had a little can of gas with him. I gladly accepted it and was on my way again in no time. I drove past another gas station but again chose not to stop. After all, the car was working, right? On and on it went. The car would work for a while, but I frequently found myself either filling up at the last minute or running out of gas on the road.

Are you with me? Re-read John 15:5.

When Christ is talking about Himself as the vine and us the branches, *this* is what He means: just like the car is designed to need fuel to run and operate, Christ also designed each of us to need *Him* to operate optimally. We have a choice to go to Him when our "tank" is three-quarters full, half-empty, or when we are completely broken down on the side of the road. We can live by the Spirit or by the flesh.

What does this mean for us?

Walking with John

I don't know about y'all, but that night, I had a huge wake-up call to stop and take time to abide in the Lord. Without abiding, I was a grouchy, irritable, impatient, frustrated, unsatisfied, ungrateful, and unloving version of myself—and it was rubbing off on Joey and those I love most.

The great news is, abiding doesn't have to take hours!

Some days, we may only have five minutes to connect with Him—and that's okay! Let's read the short devotional app on our phones before getting out of bed, or talk to Him while doing the dishes, or listen to worship music or a podcast in the car.

It's the act of turning to Him in small moments, continually throughout the day, that actually allows us to be the moms, wives, and women we want to be!

To truly love our families well, we have to be connected to the source that gives us exactly what we need.

Questions to Ponder

- How full is your "tank?"
- What is one small action you can take *today* to "fill up" with the Holy Spirit (i.e. listen to worship music or a podcast, read your Bible, take a prayer walk)?
- How can you find even five minutes each day to connect with Him?

Faith-Filled Ideas

Does your tank need to be filled today? Join me in a quick prayer:

Lord,

I need you. I'm sorry for trying to do everything myself. I wasn't designed to do this alone. I'm feeling empty, and I need you to fill me up today. Help me make time each day to abide in You. Remove the lies and distractions that keep me from turning to you as my source of strength, peace, and support. Thank you for the gift of being able to abide in You. Thank you for being the vine that provides exactly what I need in every situation. Allow me to bear fruit for Your kingdom and for my family.

I love you.

journal

_____

_____

_____

_____

_____

_____

_____

_____

_____

_____

_____

_____

_____

_____

_____

_____

_____

_____

_____

_____

_____

_____

_____

_____

_____

_____

_____

Walking with John

Spreading the *gift* of Jesus to your neighbor!

Help Club for Kids

We all know what it feels like to go through hard times, seasons, or even years. Helping our children to be aware of other people's suffering is giving them a precious gift- the gift of compassion! The Bible says in Psalm 34:18 (NIV) :

"The Lord is close to the brokenhearted and saves those who are crushed in spirit."

As we lean into the Lenten season, preparing us to remember the suffering, death and resurrection of Jesus, we should encourage our children to "put on" compassion. They should wear it like a piece of clothing as they leave our homes, to help them look at people as Jesus would have. He came to give people hope. Encourage your kids that they too, are hope-bearers!

To prepare for this activity:

1. As a family, think of a person or family in your community/circle that is going through trouble or hurting. Decide on one person/family that God brings to mind. Tell your children that you are going on "Operation Compassion" as a family!

2. Grab some sticky notes or colorful index cards from the dollar store. You will find a list of ideas on the next page, but fill as many cards as you can with words of encouragement, verses, or prayers. Have your little ones draw hearts, crosses, or anything that brings beauty to contribute.

3. Choose a day to implement your "Operation Compassion". Put it on the calendar and pray for that person or family every evening for dinner until your big day. On the day, sneakily "attack" their front door, taping or sticking the notes all over it! Keep it anonymous and feel free to leave treats or cookies, too! Your kids will have a BLAST while being a blessing.

*** *Color Printable found at myhelpclubformoms.com* ***

Spreading the *gift* of Jesus to your neighbor!

Help Club for Kids

You are victorious! God is your helper! (1 John 5:4)	We are praying for you!	God is for you! (Psalm 118:6)
God will never leave you! (Joshua 1:9)	You are loved!	Do not be troubled! (John 14:27)
God gives you everything you need! (2 Cor. 9:8)	You are a blessing to us!	God will give you peace! (Isaiah 26:3)

*** Color Printable found at myhelpclubformoms.com ***

Food for the Soul

The Lenten season has always meant a 40-day period of sacrifice or giving up something to identify with Christ and his suffering. Whether Catholic, Episcopalian, Lutheran, Reformed, Baptist, or nondenominational, we can all benefit from the season of reflection as we approach Resurrection Sunday.

My husband grew up Catholic and eating fish on Fridays during Lent was something he and his family did religiously. I didn't practice this tradition growing up, but now I enjoy honoring Jesus in this way. You don't need to adopt this into your holidays, but in case you already serve fish on Good Friday, why not try Salmon: Three Different Ways!

Salmon: Three Different Ways
PAN-SEARED GARLIC BUTTER SALMON,
PESTO & FETA SALMON, & ORANGE TERIYAKI SALMON
By: Rae-Ellen Sanders

Pan-Seared Garlic Butter Salmon is simple and delicious. Go gourmet and add white wine for a tangy twist. Use an oaky or light Chardonnay or Pinot Gris. Do not use a sweet wine. Substitute chicken broth if you choose not to use wine.

Ingredients:

1-2 pounds salmon (I prefer skinless- just one messy step to avoid), room temperature and patted dry

Salt and pepper (season both sides)

2 tablespoons butter, plus 1 tablespoon for sauce

3-6 cloves of garlic pressed fresh or use 2 teaspoons minced garlic

⅓ cup dry white wine or chicken broth

Lemon—cut in half (fresh squeezed is 100 times better than bottled)

Directions:

1. Heat a non-stick frying pan over medium heat. Add 2 tablespoons butter to the pan and heat to simmering.

2. Press garlic into butter and sauté till fragrant.

3. Raise heat to high and add the salmon fillets. If salmon has skin, cook skin-side down for three minutes. When the fish is slightly crispy, flip it over, and cook for an additional 3 minutes on the other side (you will only flip your fish once). Cooking the salmon over high heat with the garlic, salt, pepper, and butter will create a beautiful crust on the fish!

4. Check the fish using a fork towards the end of cooking. If it flakes easily, it is done. Do not overcook it, as it will also continue to cook slightly once removed from the pan. Transfer fish to a serving platter.

5. Deglaze your pan by adding the wine or broth and scraping any browned bit off the bottom of your pan. Add lemon juice and the remaining tablespoon of butter and simmer for one minute.

6. Pour butter sauce over your simple and delicious Garlic Butter Salmon and enjoy!

Note: When added to the plate, a green veggie, whether asparagus, broccoli, or string beans (check out Brandi's Bacon Green Beans in Lent Week 3) creates a colorful accompaniment.

MEAL TWO: PESTO & FETA SALMON

Pesto & Feta Salmon is an all-time favorite at our house, and it is super easy. Spoon on garlic and pesto sauce, sprinkle with feta cheese, and bake. Voila!

Ingredients:

1-2 pounds salmon (patted dry)

3-6 cloves of pressed garlic

½ cup feta cheese, crumbled

¼ cup prepared pesto

Directions:

1. Preheat oven to 400 degrees.

2. Press garlic and spread over fish.

3. Spoon pesto sauce on each filet.

4. Sprinkle feta evenly over each piece.

5. Bake for 20 minutes. *Yummo!*

Note: We've enjoyed this salmon alongside baked potatoes or salad with extra feta..

MEAL THREE: ORANGE TERIYAKI SALMON

This **Orange Teriyaki Salmon** is a tasty salmon made easy by steaming in tin foil. The foil locks in flavor and makes for easy cleanup. Take this on the road and make your next camping trip a gastronome (gourmet) experience. This can also be prepared by grilling in the woods or in your backyard. Prepare the ingredients for the Orange Teriyaki Sauce in a separate saucepan. Heat till sauce is thickened and slightly reduced. Blacken your salmon on the grill and drizzle sauce on top.

Food for the Soul

Ingredients:

1-2 pounds salmon (patted dry, sprinkled with salt and pepper)

¼ cup rice wine

¼ cup orange juice

¼ cup soy sauce

¼ cup honey

2 tablespoons sesame oil

2 teaspoons cornstarch

12-ounce bag frozen stir-fry vegetables

Directions: (for steamed version)

1. Place salmon on an ample piece of tin foil in a shallow baking dish.

2. Fold up the four sides, to prohibit leaking.

3. Combine rice wine, orange juice, soy sauce, honey, sesame oil, and cornstarch. Whisk together. Don't leave out the sesame oil—it makes all the difference!

4. Heat sauce in a separate saucepan until thickened and slightly reduced.

5. Layer frozen vegetables on top of salmon.

6. Pour sauce over fish and vegetables.

7. Seal tin foil.

8. Bake in a 400 degree oven for 30 minutes.

Serving Suggestion: Serve over Japanese noodles or white rice. Orange wedges make for an easy dessert and complete the meal.

Walking with John

~ Week Ten ~

Dear Precious Sister,

Hasn't this Lenten season been so meaningful? I love that Lent, like Advent, draws our spiritual gaze to Jesus in the Word of God! Christmas Advent anticipates the coming of the Messiah, while Lent takes us through His agonizing departure from His earthly ministry. The season keeps our intentional focus on Jesus' ultimate sacrifice on the cross, powerful resurrection that conquered sin and death, and reconciliation to God with Jesus as Lord, Savior, and Friend. That, sisters, is *glorious!*

We have been reading through the book of John and are approaching Chapters 17-20 this week. Take a few minutes to meditate on the *glory* of God:

> Now this is eternal life; that they know you, the only true God, and Jesus Christ, whom you have sent. I have brought you glory on earth by finishing the work you gave me to do. And now, Father glorify me in your presence with the glory I had with you before the world began. (John 17:3-5)

Wow, after reflecting on that simple passage of Scripture, I am overwhelmed with Jesus' omnipotence! He speaks of His unlimited power to be in the glorious presence of God the Father before creation, then to be deployed to save the human race—fully God and man to be the blood sacrifice for the forgiveness of sins—and finally to ascend after His work was done to the *glory* of Heaven. Hallelujah! These verses just about sum it *all* up!

As you continue studying the book of John and preparing for Holy Week, take time to be awed by God's glory. Amidst the bunnies and candy sales of the culture, escape to the restful place of reflection, worship, repentance, and hopeful longing. This time will affirm the hope of God's presence and the promise of His coming kingdom.

Together in reverence,
Rae-Ellen Sanders and the Help Club for Moms Team

> *Glory is the dazzling, jaw-dropping, awe-inspiring showcase of God's character to a world darkened by sin. It is the explosive radiance produced by his holiness, love, mercy, justice, wisdom, and power—all of which come together in the most fitting way in the death of Christ.*
> ~ Jeremy Treat

Mom Tips

By: Leslie Leonard

*"Let your roots grow down into him, and let your lives be built on him.
Then your faith will grow strong in the truth you were taught,
and you will overflow with thankfulness."* ~ Colossians 2:7 (NLT)

The Wise Woman Builds Her Spirit

- Drown out thoughts that oppose God's truth by memorizing Psalm 19:14. Write it on your chalkboard or a notecard to carry with you. Any time a thought pops into your mind that isn't worthy of praise, replace it with this Scripture.

- Pray in the car while doing errands or in the school pick up/drop off line. Use this time in the car to bring any concerns to the Lord. Turn off the radio and pray out loud.

The Wise Woman Loves Her Husband

- Clear any clutter from your master bedroom. Make your bedroom a peaceful, calm place that promotes relaxation and romance. Commit to putting away that last bit of laundry and removing anything that distracts or causes stress.

- Pray over your husband's car. Pray that he will arrive to and from work safely, and that his commute will be stress-free and easy. Pray that he radiates the light of Jesus in his words and actions to those around him.

The Wise Woman Loves Her Children

- If your kids are squabbling and antagonizing each other, memorize Colossians 3:12 together. Once you've memorized that, continue to memorize through the end of verse 17. Reward them with a fun treat when they do.

- Have your children take turns praying at meal times. Encourage your children to really talk to God, and to be thankful for specific blessings in their lives.

The Wise Woman Cares For Her Home

- Listen to a Help Club for Moms video while folding the laundry, sweeping the floor, or vacuuming. You can find several to choose from on our Facebook page.

- Take time this week to clean out your car. Remove all the trash and throw it away. Take out the car seats and vacuum the entire vehicle. Wipe down all the surfaces with cleaner and put away any items that do not belong in the vehicle. Restock tissues and any other items you keep in your vehicle.

> 66 In this world you will have trouble, but take heart!
> I have overcome the world. 99
> ~ John 16:33

"Savior, worthy of honor and glory
Worthy of all our praise, You overcame
Jesus, awesome in power forever
Awesome and great is Your name, You overcame
Power in hand speaking the Father's plan
You're sending us out, light in this broken land."
  ~ John Egan, *Overcome*

- Call your prayer partner for your 10-minute prayer call. If you are having trouble connecting, keep trying! If you don't have someone to pray with, ask God to bring her to you! He is faithful and will provide!

- Cherished Daughter of the Most High, come. Delight yourself in His Word today. Ask Jesus to open your eyes to His truth; your heart to a deeper understanding of the depth of His love for you. Pray, "Come Holy Spirit, speak to me." Read John 16.

Walking with John

Walking and Talking with Jesus

By: Rebekah Measmer

This beautiful passage, which is full of warnings and several promises, records the continuation of the final conversation between Jesus and His followers after the Last Supper. It is not known exactly where this conversation took place, but we know it was during the hours preceding Jesus' intense prayer in the Garden of Gethsemane. With the Crucifixion looming ahead—the excruciating details of which He would have already known—these final instructions and teaching are a testament to Jesus' selfless and loving nature. He focused on comforting His disciples and warning them of what was to come when, in fact, Jesus Himself desperately needed comforting that night. Frightened and confused by many of His warnings and vague declarations, the disciples struggled to make sense of what Jesus was saying.

Naturally, Jesus knew that His words would not be fully understood at the time, but His foresight not only demonstrated His deity but also prepared the disciples for the day when He would not be physically present. Many wonderful promises are made in this passage such as the assurance of the Holy Spirit coming as a counselor "to guide you into all truth." Jesus also promised that their grief would turn to joy and that all His followers would be "scattered," an echo of the prophecy in Zechariah: "Strike the shepherd, and the sheep will be scattered…" (Zechariah 13:7). As we know, believers were scattered to the four corners of the earth—a necessary occurrence for the Gospel to spread to all nations.

The promises of Jesus in John 16, though given to His disciples over two thousand years ago, are just as relevant today. We, as followers of Jesus, have the Holy Spirit to intercede for us, guide us, and convict us of our sin. Additionally, our grief will be turned to joy, and whatever we ask in Jesus' name, we shall receive in accordance with His will. And finally, Jesus promised that life would be hard (verse 33), but to take comfort in the fact that He, the Savior of the World, has overcome it all—suffering, death, and sin. He came to reconcile us to God so that we might have peace and relationship with Him. He, our Savior and friend, desires to walk and talk with us, comforting, counseling, and preparing us for what lies ahead.

Questions to Ponder

• After reading through this chapter of the book of John, were there any promises listed that God highlighted in your heart? Write them down!

Faith-Filled Ideas

Imagine that you're in the garden with Jesus when He is talking with His closest followers and friends. What would you have asked Him if you had been there, sitting at His feet among the disciples? Write your question down, and ask the Holy Spirit to speak to you, giving you new insight and clarity.

Journal

_____

_____

_____

_____

_____

_____

_____

_____

_____

_____

_____

_____

_____

_____

_____

_____

journal

Walking with John

> ...So that they may be brought to complete unity. Then the world will know that you sent me and have loved them even as you have loved me.
>
> ~ John 17:23

Walking with John

"To a true child of God, the invisible bond that unites all believers to Christ is far more tender, and lasting, and precious; and, as we come to recognize that we are all dwelling in one sphere of life in Him, we learn to look on every believer as our brother, in a sense that is infinitely higher than all human relationships. This is the one and only way to bring disciples permanently together. All other plans for promoting the unity of the Church have failed."
~ A.T. Pierson

- Read John 17. Highlight or underline some of the repeated ideas in this prayer, and then write them down in your own journal. Example: Jesus uses the word glory several times. Jesus prays that we would be "one."

- Think and write about why He might repeat these things.

Unified

By: Elise Turner

Every Thursday evening, I attend a service for young adults in Colorado Springs. During last Thursday's service, worship felt more like labor for me. I struggled and strained to force out what should have flown effortlessly. For a few seconds, I stopped struggling to listen to the voices around me. Though my voice was weak, altogether, we were one mighty voice floating to the Father on His throne and the Son on His right side, whom I imagined weeping with happiness, saying to the Father, "Look, the children you have given me. They are unified, in glory and belief, for they know who I am. Their praises bring us glory on the earth." This gathering is *home* for me. The people worshipping next to me, who carried my weakness that night, are my family, with God as our Father. We may not share the same last name, but we share His. We are a family similar to you, your husband, and children.

If you've never thought about your family as being representative of the family of believers and how we relate to God, think about the similarities now. You, your children, and your husband are one unit. People rarely think of you without also thinking of your children or husband. You are your individual self, but you're also who they've made you—a mom, a wife. You all belong to each other. You share one name, and the world knows you by that name. This design is no accident. God designed our relationships to reflect the way He relates to us.

John 17 states Jesus' hopes for His family, the Church, which are not far from those we have for our own families. We're getting a glimpse into Jesus' pure heart for us. This is a chapter we should tune into.

In the days before His death, in His last documented prayer, Jesus comes before the Father, pleading for unity, that believers would exemplify the interdependent relationship of the Godhead: "I pray...that all of them may be one" (John 17:21).

In this single prayer, Jesus prays "that they [the believers] may be one as we are one" three times (John 17:11b; 21; 22). He is asking that we would be bonded in the same way He and the Father are bonded. Just like in a family, the members of Christ's Body function optimally when we rely on and complement each other, love each other, and understand each other's minds and hearts.

He follows His pleas for unity with a "so that" clause: "So that the world may believe you have sent me" (John 17:21b), implying that the former would result in the latter. In other words, if we are unified, the world will know that we really do belong to Jesus, that He is who He says He is, and that His love is freely given to those who believe. How the world sees Jesus depends on how unified we are.

The Church on Earth can only aspire to the level of unity of the triune God. However, if we are surprised by Jesus' emphasis on unity, then it's time for us to realign our desires to those of Jesus, honoring His departing wishes for His blood-bought family.

Questions to Ponder

• How can I care for other believers in the same way I care for my children and husband?

• What does my family show me about unity that I can apply to my relationships with people outside of my family?

Faith-Filled Ideas

Think about other women you are connected to, and how you can increase unity with them. You might ask someone what she needs prayer for and pray fiercely for that issue like it's your own. The more you pray for this person, the more you will care for and understand her. Or, maybe you can think of a situation in which setting aside your pride would benefit that particular relationship. Sometimes, we have to choose to love and serve someone simply because he or she also belongs to Jesus.

journal

Walking with John

journal

_____

_____

_____

_____

_____

_____

_____

_____

_____

_____

_____

_____

_____

_____

_____

_____

_____

_____

_____

_____

_____

_____

_____

_____

_____

_____

_____

_____

Walking with John

"For you will certainly carry out God's purpose, however you act, but it makes a difference to you whether you serve like Judas or like John."
~ C.S. Lewis, *The Problem of Pain*

- It's time to meet with your Jesus! Whether it's in your comfy chair with a cup of coffee or at the kitchen table before the kiddos awake, there is never a wrong way to spend time with Jesus.

- Read John 18, allowing the Holy Spirit to reveal His message directly to you. Write John 18:37 in your journal.

Walking with John

A Matter of Grace

By: Shelly Wright

Our study of John so far, through chapter 17, has been about the life of Jesus. However, in chapter 18, John takes a sharp turn. This is where Jesus' ministry, miracles, and relationships with His disciples end and the road to the cross begins—with one kiss. Matthew 26:48-49 says, "Now the betrayer had arranged a signal with them: 'The one I kiss is the man; arrest him.' Going at once to Jesus, Judas said, 'Greetings, Rabbi!' and kissed him."

Have you ever wondered why Jesus chose Judas to be part of the elite twelve, knowing Judas would betray Him?

The Holy Spirit entered my life in the fall of 1998 when I was 26 years old. Soon after that, I married the love of my life and a year later I became a mom. Another year later, while six months pregnant with my second child, God spoke to me. He wanted me to start VBS in my church. Never having led anything my entire life, I was terrified (and hormonal).

Jeremiah 29:11 says, "'For I know the plans I have for you,' declares the Lord, 'plans to prosper you and not to harm you, plans to give you hope and a future.'"

I followed God's call, serving as VBS Director for eleven years. Even though it was such an amazing calling, it wasn't an easy one. I've dealt with various issues over those years, but the most difficult part was holding my team members accountable. To be fair, I tend to give 110% in anything I commit to—volunteer or not—and I expected the same out of my team. As you can imagine, my expectations weren't always taken well. Some volunteers refused to serve under me, while I watched others flourish.

What does this have to do with Judas?

Everything Jesus did in the flesh, He wanted us to mirror. He selected the twelve disciples to carry out His will, knowing He would be deceived by Judas. Jesus extended grace over and over again to Judas. Matthew 5:44 says, "But I tell you, love your enemies and pray for those who persecute you." Judas hardened his heart and eventually, the truth came out the moment he kissed Jesus' cheek.

1 Corinthians 4:5 says, "Therefore judge nothing before the appointed time; wait until the Lord comes. He will bring to light what is hidden in darkness and will expose the motives of the heart. At that time, each will receive their praise from God."

Whether we face difficult people in our children's schooling, church fellowships, or daily lives, we are required to extend grace—overlook offensive behavior—so they experience the love of God in action. Didn't Jesus die for that very reason? Just as He extended grace toward us while we were still sinners, He wants us to be graceful with others *because* they don't deserve it. It seems foolish that Jesus would keep Judas in His tight group of men, knowing he was a traitor. Yet, He continued to bless him. Unlike Jesus, we don't know someone's heart. Maybe the person we think is a Judas is really a John in the making.

**DISCLAIMER: Extending grace works for most situations, but not all. Obviously, there are more serious situations in which you may need help to deal with someone's behavior. You could get support from your husband, church leaders, or even law enforcement. Seek counsel if you are distressed or fearful in an encounter or relationship.

Questions to Ponder

- Do you feel God has abandoned you? Read Jeremiah 29:11 again. Ask God to reveal His plans for your life.
- According to John 18:1-14, what was Jesus' response to the soldiers?
- Is there someone you struggle to be friends with? Pray and ask God to help you. If it's a destructive relationship, pray 1 Corinthians 4:5 for God to expose motives.

Faith-Filled Ideas

If you believe and have received Jesus as your personal Savior, invite an unbeliever you know to your Easter Sunday service. Many unchurched people will attend a special holiday event, so take this opportunity to reach out to them. It may be the beginning of their journey to Christ.

If you have never prayed to receive Jesus Christ as your personal Savior, it's as easy as **A, B, C: A**dmit to God you're a sinner (Romans 3:23). **B**elieve that Jesus is God's Son (John 3:16). **C**onfess your faith in Jesus as your Lord and Savior (Romans 10:9).

Walking with John

journal

_____

_____

_____

_____

_____

_____

journal

Walking with John

Observing *Passover*

Help Club for Kids

It is such a blessing to observe Passover as a Christian family! My family honors the Jewish feasts and we have started passing on the fun ways we celebrate.

The Passover Seder means- "order" and, at a traditional Seder, the ceremony follows a precise order. It is lengthy-to say the least. Every mama knows that with small kids who want to participate, you need a tangible idea to keep their minds focused.

This page and the next, will give you a few ideas to help you observe, while having fun! Honoring times when God saved His people is sure to bring special memories year after year. We pray that observing Passover becomes a sweet tradition in your home.

Walking with John

Red Paper Chain

Passover Paper-Chain Craft- this craft is easy and affordable. Scissors, glue and red construction paper is all you'll need! You can either print the Scriptures, cut & glue them or write them out with a marker. These verses reiterate God's command to commemorate this ceremony annually. In remembrance, hang your paper chain over your front door to represent the blood of The Lamb.

| Exodus 12:14 | Exodus 12:17 | Exodus 12:26-27 | Exodus 13:3 | Matthew 26:28 |

*** *Color Printable found at myhelpclubformoms.com* ***

Observing *Passover*

Decorate a "Red Sea" Themed Table

Then Moses stretched out his hand over the sea, and the Lord drove the sea back by a strong east wind all night and made the sea dry land, and the waters were divided. Exodus 14:21

Decorate your table with a Red Sea theme. It will make the Seder dinner memorable but also captivate your children and guests' attention.

Gather up as many Lego and Playmobile figures as you can and recreate the miraculous crossing right down the middle of your table! If you don't have boys in your house, mini dolls and figures can also work. Be creative with construction paper, dollar store plastic tablecovers, sand, sea shells, glitter (whatever your mama creativity can handle).

The most important part of this re-creation is the re-telling! Make sure to read the Passover and Israelites escape from slavery from Egypt in

Exodus 12:1-30 and Exodus 14:1-31.

*** Color Printable found at myhelpclubformoms.com ***

Passover

By: Rae-Ellen Sanders

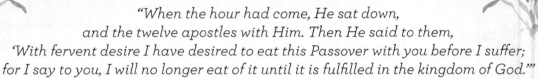

"When the hour had come, He sat down,
and the twelve apostles with Him. Then He said to them,
'With fervent desire I have desired to eat this Passover with you before I suffer;
for I say to you, I will no longer eat of it until it is fulfilled in the kingdom of God.'"

~Luke 22:14-16 (NKJV)

"The Lord kept the Passover with His disciples in the Upper Room to fulfill the law. More than that, communion with Him looks toward the Wedding Supper that we will be eating and drinking in the last days. Jesus fulfilled the Old Covenant by His observance of the Pesach (Passover) and at the same time established the New Covenant with us. We entered into a new dimension of worship and fellowship with the spirit. Jesus was about to be sacrificed as the Passover Lamb. We are not only to observe the Lord's Supper, we are to be a part of it by being part of His sacrificed body. Jesus participated and finished the old ceremony that we might participate with Him and be a part of the new." ~ Author unknown

My family and I had the privilege of hosting a Seder dinner and also attending another at our church this year. It was exciting to research our Hebraic roots and see how Jesus is tied into Passover. So many Christians don't understand Passover or the significance it holds to Resurrection Sunday. I would like to share what I learned. Following are instructions of how you would perform a Seder dinner in your own home. I hope learning about how the Jews celebrate Passover will encourage you to see their devotion and how they look to the Messiah for redemption! There is a lot of Scripture reading so be prepared to turn some pages! Grab your Bible and a notebook to take notes and get cozy.

Passover commemorates the Israelites departure from Egypt into freedom from slavery. You can read about it in Exodus when the Lord instructed the Israelites, the night they escaped Pharaoh's rule, to kill a spotless lamb and paint the blood over their doorpost. It would be a sign for the death angel to *pass over* their homes and protect their firstborn sons from the tenth plague (Exodus 12:13). Pharaoh comes to his breaking point when his son is killed and tells Moses his people can go! In haste, they eat their bread and lamb while standing, then flee to the Red Sea where they experience God's deliverance. I highly recommend reading the account Exodus 13:17-14:31 for yourself.

Every year at Passover (Pesach), Jews sit down to retell this story with many prayers, blessings, cups of wine, and a special ceremonial dinner that commemorates the Exodus. "Seder," which means "order," is so named because of the specific order of events followed in this deliverance celebration. The celebration is pretty long but it's important that you don't skip any steps, it's like a dress rehearsal. Every step and blessing is imperative to the Passover celebration. The quoted blessings are to be spoken out loud by the man of the household.

Pesach is actually a lasting ordinance performed every year. It is first instructed in Scripture in Exodus 12:1-28 and then ordained by God in Leviticus 23.

Passover

By: Rae-Ellen Sanders

So this day shall be to you a memorial; and you shall keep it as a feast
to the Lord throughout your generations. You shall keep it as a feast by an
everlasting ordinance. (Exodus 12:14)

The difference from the first Passover is that you sit comfortably in relaxation or lean on pillows rather than eating in a hurry. Passover begins with the woman of the house lighting a candle that represents her bringing "light" into the world through childbirth as Mary did with Jesus, "The Light of The World." The candle also signifies that Christ will bring us out of darkness. She says a prayer that starts the Passover Celebration.

During the meal, five cups of wine are served to each individual. Each cup of wine is served with an accompanying Scripture and symbolizes an expression of God's redemption for His people.

A blessing and a prayer of sanctification accompany **The First Cup** of wine. "I will bring you out from under the burdens of the Egyptians and deliver you from bondage" (Exodus 6:6 NKJV). For the Christian, the first cup represents God's promise to deliver us from the bondage of this world, setting us apart for a life of holiness.

At this time, participants ritually wash their hands and feet before partaking of the meal. "Wash yourselves, make yourselves clean; remove the evil of your deeds from My sight"(Isaiah 1:16). This is a spiritual act of setting oneself apart for the works of God. Christ shows us through the example of washing the disciples feet to serve each other and to bear each other's burdens. Read John 13:4-5, Isaiah 52:7, and John 13:12-17 out loud while washing one another's feet.

On the table is a large plate with five symbols of the Passover on it; "bitter herbs," usually horseradish; a "vegetable," usually parsley; "Chazeret," often romaine lettuce; "Charoset," a mixture of apples, nuts, and cinnamon; and a "Shankbone" from a lamb. In addition there is a bowl of salt water, three Matzah pieces wrapped in linen, a wine glass, and an extra place setting with cup and chair for the spirit of Elijah, the forerunner of the coming of the Messiah.

Next, a piece of parsley is dipped into salt water and eaten, to remind the Jewish people that life in Egypt before Passover was filled with tears (salt water). Read Matthew 26:21-25.

The patriarch takes out the middle piece of Matzah (unleavened bread) and breaks it into two pieces. The larger piece is then hidden until the end of the meal. The other piece is added back to the white linen.

As Christians, we understand the three pieces of the bread to represent the Trinity; Father, Son, and Holy Spirit, three co-equal persons of the Godhead, all without corruption (leaven). The white linen represents Their heavenly abode which is pure and holy. The Matzah is striped with holes in it, foreshadowing the pierced, broken Jesus. The middle piece symbolizes the Bread of Life (Jesus) to all those who partake of Him. At the completion of the meal, the children will look for the hidden piece called the "Afikomen" (a Greek word meaning "He came" or "dessert"; to bring out that which is hidden). It is returned to the linen with the other pieces. This points to the resurrection and ascension. The child who finds the

Passover

By: Rae-Ellen Sanders

Afikomen is rewarded. Likewise, we are rewarded with the indwelling of the Holy Spirit and eternity fellowshipping with our God when we accept Christ as Lord and Savior!

The Passover story is then read from Exodus 12:1-14. The youngest at the table asks the following questions at every Seder meal and they are answered by the dad or man of the house with these words.

- *"Why is this night different from all other nights?*
  "Because on every Passover night, including tonight, we repeat the call that echoed through the entrance of Pharaohs palace: Let My people go!"

- *"On all other nights, we may eat leavened bread or Matzah, but on this night, why do we only eat unleavened bread?"*
  "Matzah reminds us that when the Jews left the slavery of Egypt, they had no time to bake their bread. They took the raw dough on their journey and baked it in the hot desert sun into hard crackers called Matzah."

- *"On all other nights, we may eat any kind of herbs, but on this night, why only bitter herbs?"*
  "Maror (bitter herbs) reminds us of the bitter and cruel way Pharaoh treated the Jewish people when they were slaves in Egypt."

- *"On all other nights, we do not dip even once, but on this night, why twice?"*
  "We dip bitter herbs into the Charoset to remind us how hard the Jewish slaves worked in Egypt. The chopped apples and nuts look like the clay bricks used in building Pharaoh's buildings."

- *"Why do we dip parsley into salt water?*
  "The parsley reminds us that Spring is here and new life will grow. The salt water reminds us of the tears of the Jewish slaves."

- *"On all other nights, we eat and drink either sitting or leaning, but on this night, why do we all lean?"*
  "We lean on a pillow to be comfortable and to remind us that once we were slaves, but now we are free!"

During the reading, it is tradition to also review the ten plagues. After each is read, you dip a finger in wine and tap it on the plate. This is done because even the suffering of our enemies pains us and God Himself is grieved at wickedness.

Psalms 113-114 are read out loud and followed by **The Second Cup** of wine, "I will set you free" represents judgment or instruction. "I will redeem you with an outstretched arm and with great judgment" (Exodus 6:6b NKJV). For the Christian, Passover is the Gospel story. The outstretched arms of Jesus on the cross demonstrated His love and sacrifice that redeemed us from our sins. Likewise, Moses' outstretched arm over the Red Sea meant deliverance for God's chosen people to freedom.

Passover

By: Rae-Ellen Sanders

The broken piece of Matzah is then taken out again and broken into smaller pieces to be distributed to each person at the table. Read Isaiah 53:5 and Matthew 26:26-29. Bitter herbs are dipped in the Charoset to remind them that even the most bitter of circumstances can be sweetened by hope in God. Read Isaiah 53:3-4. The Shankbone is a remnant of the lamb that provided the blood so God would pass over their homes (Exodus 12:21-22). For some, the Paschal (Passover) lamb would have been expensive, so families would share a lamb between them. A tiny piece of meat is used in a "binding sandwich" with Matzah and bitter herb. This small morsel is eaten just before a regular meal is served.

After eating to satisfaction, the much awaited time for children to search for the Afikomen begins. When it is found, a gift is given and dessert is enjoyed. (At this point you might think the Seder is over, but it is not! Be prepared for a long celebration!) There are still two more cups of wine to drink. (At our Seder, we used cranberry juice).

The Third Cup of wine, "I will redeem you", is the Cup of Blessing or Redemption, known to the Jews as the "Communion" Cup. Read Mark 14:22-25, Luke 22:19-20, and 1 Corinthians 11:23-26. The wine in this cup is the color of blood. Before drinking, take one last piece of Matzah, a part of the one that was hidden, and recite, "This is my body which is given for you; do this in remembrance of Me." Partake of both the Matzah and the wine in communion. Read John 14:27-31 as a final blessing.

The last cup will now be filled to overflowing. (It's a good idea to have a plate underneath). The overflowing cup represents the Promised Land flowing with milk and honey. For believers in Christ, this promised land is Heaven. This cup is for Elijah, the hoped-for guest who will sit at the table with a place ready for him. The door is even left ajar so he can enter the room easily. Often in Jewish homes, the children will search for him. Elijah's arrival precipitates the coming of the Messiah, hence the excitement.

One more cup, **The Fourth Cup** of wine, "I will take you as my people", is the Cup of Praise or Hope, also known as the Cup for the Wedding Feast of the Lamb. "I will bring you to the land which I swore to give to Abraham, Isaac, and to Jacob, and I will give it to you for a possession; I am the LORD" (Isaiah 6:8). It exemplifies the future fulfillment of all of God's promises.

The Third and Fourth Cups of the Seder are the Betrothed and Wedding Cups of the New Covenant. The Fourth Cup, "I will take you to me" is what happens when two people get married. The cups parallel the wedding betrothal process in ancient Jewish custom. When a man proposed, he would negotiate a bride price. (Jesus paid the Bride price when He died for us and rose again). The man would hand the bride a cup of wine and say, "This is the cup of my covenant." (Jesus said these exact words at the Last Supper). If she drank, it meant, "I do", and then at the wedding, they would drink another cup of wine together.

When Jesus says, "I will not drink of this fruit of the vine until I drink it anew with you in My Father's Kingdom," He is connecting this future cup with the cup He drank that night at the Last Supper. The disciples, familiar with the Seder, understood exactly what He meant by that connection. Jesus will come back for His Bride to have the Last Cup together!

Passover

By: Rae-Ellen Sanders

To conclude the Seder, many sing in worship; Psalm 115, 118 and 136 are often sung. Passover ends with the words: ***"Next year in Jerusalem."***

As you can see, we have more in common with our Jewish brothers and sisters than you may have thought! The ritual of Passover can be celebrated by both Christians and Jews. For the chosen people, it is a testament to God's faithful deliverance from human bondage through Moses. For grafted-in believers, it affirms God's miraculous providence throughout history to release us from the bondage of sin through our Savior, Jesus Christ!

_____
_____
_____
_____
_____
_____
_____
_____
_____
_____
_____
_____
_____
_____
_____

Walking with John

~ Week Eleven ~

Sweet Sister,

The heart-wrenching events of that first Holy Week fulfilled prophecies penned by prophets thousands of years before. From the beginning of time, it was God's plan to save and deliver His beloved creation—you and me. The brutal whipping, the questioning, the mocking, the crucifixion, and the supernatural resurrection of Jesus changed our destiny from eternal death and damnation to everlasting *life* and peace. This die-for-you love, this beautiful, new reality is available still today, to "whosoever believes"!

Your sins are forever paid for! Though Jesus died over two thousand years ago, His pure blood stands eternal. It *still* washes and makes new; even to this day it is alive, working miracles!

Hallelujah!

Open your heart wide this week to receive the complete work of our wonderful Savior. Allow Him to have His way, to do what only He can do. Abundant life comes through no other name. Let the reality of the cross tangibly touch the impossibilities you're facing. You are loved, more than you could ever know.

Blessings and love,
Mari Jo Mast and the Help Club For Moms Team

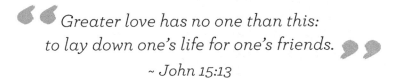

Greater love has no one than this:
to lay down one's life for one's friends.
~ John 15:13

Mom Tips

By: Leslie Leonard

"Let your roots grow down into him, and let your lives be built on him. Then your faith will grow strong in the truth you were taught, and you will overflow with thankfulness." ~ Colossians 2:7 (NLT)

The Wise Woman Builds Her Spirit

- Challenge yourself to memorize a Bible verse this week: Record it on your phone or write it on index cards and place them around your home and car (inside cupboards, by the washing machine, on the bathroom mirror, on your dashboard). Keep practicing saying it out loud until you have it memorized.

- Pray with your prayer partner this week. If you are having trouble connecting, keep trying until you get to pray. It's worth the effort!

The Wise Woman Loves Her Husband

- Find little ways to show love to your husband: bring him something to drink and a snack while he is relaxing in the evening, hang up his clothes for him when he returns home from work, or make his favorite treat just for him. One of the most meaningful ways to show love is in the small things done consistently.

- Pray every day that your husband would experience such love for God that his heart would overflow with worship. Journal about your insights into yourself and your husband.

The Wise Woman Loves Her Children

- Journal about each of your children's characteristics right now. Mark this moment in time because as they grow and change, you will want to look back at what they were like at certain ages. Write about their likes and dislikes, what you love about them, what they do that makes you laugh, messes they made, etc.

- Teach your children a new praise song this week. Choose a simple chorus that is easy for all ages to learn. Practice while they ride with you in the car. Remind your children that singing is a form of worship. You can reference Psalm 100.

The Wise Woman Cares For Her Home

- Dust all the blinds in your home this week. Vacuum out the windowsills and wipe down the baseboards. If you have curtains, vacuum the curtains to remove any dust.

- Choose one day to clean out your refrigerator. Remove everything and discard the spoiled or expired items. Wipe down the entire fridge and put everything back in an organized manner.

> Jesus knew that his mission was now finished, and to fulfill Scripture he said,
> 'I am thirsty.' A jar of sour wine was sitting there, so they soaked a sponge in it,
> put it on a hyssop branch, and held it up to his lips. When Jesus had tasted it,
> he said, 'It is finished!' Then he bowed his head and gave up his spirit.
>
> ~ John 19:28-29 (NLT)

"All change comes from deepening your understanding of the salvation of Christ and living out the changes that understanding creates in your heart."
~ Tim Keller

- Call your prayer partner for your 10-minute prayer call. Keep trying to connect until you get to pray together. This tiny habit of praying with a friend regularly will truly change your life!

- Sweet Mom, creation was, is, and will be forever changed because of one single act of unconditional love from our eternal Savior. Although we don't deserve one ounce of grace, Jesus paid the price of our debt and offers eternal life to those who trust in Him.

- Read John 19.

Walking with John

It Is Finished!

By: Mari Jo Mast

Every time I read the events which lead up to Christ's crucifixion, my heart bleeds and emphatically cries out, "NO!!!!" It just isn't fair! Don't they know He isn't guilty and doesn't deserve to die? Can't they understand He's the God who came to save them? Accusations spill out of my judgmental heart. I mean, surely if I had lived back then, I would have known He was God's Son!

However, as I continue to read, my heart turns soft. It becomes all too clear; it was God's plan for the innocent Son of Man and Son of God to be crucified. Jesus knew at a young age His heavenly purpose: To die a brutal, substitutionary death in payment of the debt disobedience had accrued. Sin had separated God from His creation, but Jesus paid the sin debt to bring restoration: perfection for imperfection. This was God's plan from the beginning, before the foundation of the world. (1 Peter 1:19-21; Ephesians 3:9-11). Eternal life is now available because Jesus suffered and died. Without His sacrifice, the Holy Spirit could not indwell believers, breathing His glory into their emptiness (Romans 8:15).

Isaiah prophesied in detail about this life-altering event, years before it happened:

> He was oppressed and treated harshly, yet He never said a word. He was led like a lamb to the slaughter. And as a sheep is silent before the shearers, he did not open his mouth. Unjustly condemned, he was led away. No one cared that he died without descendants, that his life was cut short in midstream. But he was struck down for the rebellion of my people. He had done no wrong and had never deceived anyone. But he was buried like a criminal; he was put in a rich man's grave. But it was the Lord's good plan to crush him and cause him grief. Yet when his life is made an offering for sin, he will have many descendants. He will enjoy a

long life, and the Lord's good plan will prosper in his hands. When he sees all that is accomplished by his anguish, he will be satisfied. And because of his experience, my righteous servant will make it possible for many to be counted righteous, for he will bear all their sins. (Isaiah 53:7-11 NLT)

My heart did a 180 from my first reaction to the cross. Not only was Jesus' sacrifice planned and prophesied, but it was also necessary because of me, my sin; I'm as guilty as those who crucified Him!

> Yet it was our weaknesses he carried; it was our sorrows that weighed him down. And we thought his troubles were a punishment from God, a punishment for his own sins! But He was pierced for our rebellion, crushed for our sins. He was beaten so we could be whole. He was whipped so we could be healed. All of us like sheep, have gone astray. We have left God's paths to follow our own. Yet the Lord laid on him the sins of us all. (Isaiah 53:4-6 NLT)

My friend, this is for you and me. Jesus' perfect blood was shed to save us two thousand years ago. His blood still saves today, and tomorrow it will continue and not stop until He returns. This is the good news of the Gospel of Jesus!

It is finished; it was enough. Hallelujah, what a Savior!

With tears in my eyes and a fervent heart of gratitude, all I can say is, "Thank you, Jesus."

Questions to Ponder

• Why did Jesus die? Do a word study in the Greek language on the word "salvation." Write down all the things Jesus paid for. Thank Him.

Faith-Filled Ideas

Keep in the forefront of your heart and mind the incredible love Jesus had when He died for you. Share it with your children.

Ask Jesus to fill you with the courage to spread The Good News of the Gospel. Pray for opportunities to share with someone who may not yet know about the great, great love of Jesus.

journal

_____

_____

_____

_____

_____

_____

_____

_____

journal

"I came to think of God as more of a gracious friend who was accompanying me on this journey, a friend who wanted to carry my burdens and speak into my life and shape me into who I really was and who I would become."
~ Joanna Gaines, *The Magnolia Story*

- Come, Sweet Mama, and rest with the Lord this morning. Grab your favorite beverage, Bible, and journal.

- Please read John 20 and write out any verses that stand out to you. Make sure to write the second half of verse 17 in your journal. Underline or circle the word 'your.'

He Calls You by Name

By: Susan Proctor

Relationships are inescapable. God had the first relationship—with Himself! Genesis 1:26 hints at the Trinity when God says, "Let us make man in Our image..." And, being made in the image of God, we are made for relationship. Casually or intimately, we need each other. Our relational God wants to know us and be known by us, speaking of Himself as our Father, Daddy, and Friend. To get as close to us as possible, He became human and lived among us. Jesus was all about people. His ministry began by establishing an inner circle of companions, then expanded to serve anyone He encountered. John 20:11-18 records a beautiful moment with His friend, Mary:

Mary had gone to the tomb of Jesus when she discovered His body was missing. The man she presumed to be the gardener asked her why she was crying. When she told Him, He said, "Mary." I absolutely love how Jesus calls Mary by her name. He doesn't go through a roll call like I do with my children. He knows Mary's heart and understands why she is crying; yet, He takes the time to hear her. As Jesus utters her name, she knows instantly who He is. Out of love and relief, she wants to cling to Him, but He explains that His mission isn't complete. Jesus will be "ascending to My Father and *your* Father—to My God and *your* God" (John 20:17). Jesus reiterates the purpose of His death on the cross and subsequent resurrection was to restore fellowship between God and His children; not only fellowship, but an intimate relationship as our Father and our God. God has relentlessly, sacrificially pursued us, and now, we must pursue Him. Jesus was an example of seeking His Father. Often, we read in the Gospels that Jesus would go to a solitary place and pray (Mark 1:35). We must find time daily to deepen our relationship with God by praying.

Sweet friend, God's heart for us isn't just to save us from our judgment, but to abide with us in a loving relationship. God yearns to be with us. He loves us more than we can imagine (Ephesians 3:17-18). He desires for us to draw near to Him (James 4:8). He wants to walk through the fire and the water with us (Isaiah 43:2). He wants to rejoice with us (Zephaniah 3:17). Basically, He wants to be with us through the good, the bad, and the ugly.

There are many benefits of having a genuine relationship with Jesus. First, we see Jesus is right there beside Mary as she is distraught over His body missing. Second, Jesus calls us by our name. He knows us. In fact, Isaiah 49:16 says that we are "inscribed" on the palms of God's hands. Third, Jesus' presence brings peace in the middle of uncertainty. Several times Jesus says, "Peace be with you" in John 20.

To be honest, right now in my life, I am grappling with a sick child. My oldest child has recently been diagnosed with an autonomic nervous system dysfunction. Almost daily, I go before the Lord looking for strength and courage to fight this crazy battle. Daily, God infuses me with His strength and fights my battles (Exodus 14:14). When Kaleb's illness began, I was overwhelmed! I had no idea what to do next. In my prayer time, God gently reminded me that He has directed my path with each new doctor, new diagnosis, and new medicine. It is only because of my relationship with God that I have been able to wade through all of the medical chaos. Kaleb isn't healed—yet. But I do have the peace and courage to get through each day, and make the most of every encounter with people (Ephesians 5:15-16).

Questions to Ponder

· What can you do to make your relationship with God more intimate?

· When my oldest son was two he would call me "Honey" because his dad did. What are some nicknames you call God? Why? For example, I call God my Abba because I never had a Dad.

Faith-Filled Ideas

Seek to find out the names of those who serve you at the grocery store, restaurant, or bank. Memorize their names and use it when you see them. Look them in the eye and make sure they know they matter.

If talking to God is difficult, pray the Lord's Prayer in Matthew 6:9-13 several times this week.

journal

_____

_____

_____

_____

_____

_____

_____

_____

_____

_____

journal

_____

_____

_____

_____

_____

_____

_____

_____

_____

_____

_____

_____

_____

_____

_____

_____

_____

_____

_____

_____

_____

_____

_____

_____

_____

_____

_____

Walking with John

"I am the subject of depression so fearful that I hope none of you ever get to such extremes of wretchedness as I go to. But I always get back again by this—I know that I trust Christ. I have no reliance but in him, and if he falls, I shall fall with him. But if he does not, I shall not. Because he lives, I shall live also, and I spring to my legs again and fight with my depressions of spirit and get the victory through it. And so may you do, and so you must, for there is no other way of escaping from it."
~ Charles H. Spurgeon

- It's time to meet with your Jesus! He is the One who loves you and has *great* things in store for your life.
- Read John 21:1-25. Ask the Holy Spirit to reveal unresolved failure or emotional pain. Imagine yourself like Peter, running to Jesus even though he had failed.

To Whom Shall We Go?

By: Deb Weakly

Do you ever feel like you have made so many mistakes in your life that your situation is hopeless, and even too far gone for God? Perhaps you have given up because there's no way it's ever going to get better.

I know how you feel, dear one, and I have felt the feelings of despair at two in the morning. I have heard the whispers of the evil enemy of our souls in the middle of the night telling me to take my own life, saying there is no use to keep going because my situation is truly hopeless.

After coming through the valley of despair, I can honestly tell you that I am so glad that I didn't listen to the accuser and give in to the dark thoughts. By the grace of God, I am here to tell you that all you have to do is hold onto Christ for dear life, trusting Him to carry you through the difficult season. Just like the pilgrims who passed through the valley of Baca and changed it into springs, so must you (Psalm 84:6).

We are not the only ones who may feel like we have made a mess out of our lives. All we have to do is look at the disciple Peter.

Peter knew what it was like to fail miserably. He had known Jesus intimately for three years as a member of His inner circle. Peter vowed his faithful, undying love to Jesus, and seemed destined for greatness. He had faith to move mountains. Jesus even called him "the rock" on whose faith He would build His church. In spite of his passion, Peter still turned away from Jesus, denying Him during the hour of His greatest need. Yes, Peter failed miserably.

As we read the story in Luke 22:54-62, we witness the heartbreaking account of Peter denying Jesus three times. After he had sinned, "he went out and wept bitterly."

This is the moment I can relate to the most: Peter crying bitter tears as he abandoned his Lord. I am sure he felt he was too far gone for God, without hope. After all of those laudatory words spoken over him by Jesus about being the foundation of His church, he was sure he missed his chance; it was all over. But as we turn a few pages to John 20, we see that Peter never lost his hope. He knew to whom he should go.

He knew to go to Jesus, his friend, and so must you.

When you look at your life, all in shambles and shame, you must set your heart and mind on Christ Jesus—not on sin, mistakes, doubt, depression, anger, bitterness, or unforgiveness. You must run to Jesus just as Peter did.

In John 20:4-6, Peter and John *ran* to the empty tomb to find Jesus. Even though John, "the disciple whom Jesus loved", got there first, it was Peter who went right in. He wanted to find Jesus.

In our reading today in John 21, we see Peter's reaction when he realizes that it is Jesus on the beach. The moment after John said, "It is the Lord," he wasted no time jumping into the water to get back to his Lord. He knew who would heal him of his guilt and shame.

Peter knew the loving and forgiving heart of Jesus who was already cooking breakfast for him and his friends on the beach. He knew that the same God providing for his physical hunger would also give him the forgiveness, love, and acceptance his heart so desperately needed.

We behold the scene in John 21:15-19 as Jesus reinstates Peter back into his calling and His love. He ends the discourse with the powerful admonishment, "Follow me!"

Dear sister, if you feel you have made a hot mess out of your life, don't pull away from Jesus. Follow Him! Instead of listening to the voice of the accuser telling you there is no hope for you, run, run, *run* to Jesus! Tell Him you are sorry, and surrender your life and your circumstances to Him. Trust that He is with you, will never leave you, and has good things in store for your life. There is always hope with Jesus. Watch Him take the broken fragments of your life and make them into something beautiful. It's what He does best!

Questions to Ponder

• What is Jesus speaking to you today?

• Is there any area of your life where you feel as if you have failed?

• Open your hands as a sign of surrender and pray; ask Jesus to take your failures and your shame. Seek forgiveness where appropriate. Imagine Jesus taking your sins and regrets, throwing them as far as the east is from the west (Psalm 103:12). Then, imagine Him holding you and telling you that He loves you, is with you, and has great plans for your life. Ask Him to help you to visualize Him turning your ashes into a crown of beauty (Isaiah 61:3).

Faith-Filled Ideas

Read John 21 to your kids from a children's version of the Bible, or one that's easy to read such as the New International Reader's Version (NIRV). Talk to your children about the importance of running to Jesus when they make mistakes; He will always help them and has great plans for their lives. Children need the hope that Jesus brings more than we could ever know, especially your children who carry shame for getting into trouble frequently. Remind these precious ones that Jesus loves them and that you love them, no matter what! Teach them from a young age to trust in Jesus and His great love for them; He will help them to do what is right.

Walking with John

journal

Walking with John

Food for the Soul

"He is not here; he has risen, just as he said. Come and see the place where he lay."
~Matthew 28:6

Here is a fun and tangible way to teach your children about the resurrection. These are a wonderful treat for Easter Saturday or Resurrection Sunday.

RESURRECTION ROLLS   By: Jennifer Valdois

Ingredients:

8 large marshmallows
½ stick of butter, melted

2 tablespoons sugar
1 teaspoons cinnamon

Directions:

1. Preheat the oven to 375 degrees.

2. Read John 19:38-42 to your children. Explain to them what each ingredient represents.
   - The marshmallow represents Jesus, white and pure because He was without sin.
   - The crescent dough represents the linen cloth they wrapped Jesus in.
   - The butter is like the embalming oils.
   - The cinnamon and sugar are like the spices they used to prepare His body for burial.

3. Spread out the crescent dough according to package directions. Melt the butter. Mix the cinnamon and sugar in a shallow bowl. Dip a marshmallow in the butter. Roll it in the cinnamon and sugar mixture. Place the marshmallow in the triangle of dough and wrap the marshmallow completely. Pinch the dough to make sure it is sealed. Dip it in the butter again to keep it from sticking to the pan.

4. Place the rolls in a muffin tin. Put the rolls in the oven, which represents the tomb, and bake for 11-13 minutes.

5. While they are baking, read John 20:1-18.

6. Open the tomb, and immediately remove the rolls from the pan to prevent them from sticking to the pan.

7. When they are cool, let your children discover what happened to the marshmallows.

He is risen, indeed!

"*Jesus*
did many other things as well.
If every one of them were
written down,
I suppose that even the
whole world
would not have room
for the books that would be
written."

~ John 21:25

Love Your Husband

~ CHALLENGE ~

Love Your Husband

CHALLENGE

~ Week Twelve ~

Dear Mama,

Marriage is such a beautiful gift from the Lord! But our fleshly hearts sometimes make a mess of beautiful gifts. Nagging notions of worry that we may not have married the right man can creep into our minds and begin to take hold of our thoughts. We wonder if perhaps we were too young, have changed too much, don't get along as well as we used to, or didn't know each other well enough from the start. We can begin to doubt that our husband is really our "soulmate."

Sister, may I speak some kind words of wisdom from a fellow mama who has been married a decade and a half and has had a mix of both good years and hard? Let me tell you this...when you married your husband, he became the *right* one for you! He is the one that you are meant to spend the rest of your life learning to love the way Jesus loves you.

You do not have to wonder anymore if God had something better for you. Your husband is God's best for you right now and for the remainder of your days on this earth. If you will allow Him, our loving Father will gently use your marriage to show you His love, to refine you, and to make you into the beautiful daughter of the King that He intended you to be.

God wants to use you in your husband's life to teach him about the love of Christ. You are a messenger of the Gospel of peace to your husband. But guess what this requires: dying to yourself. Do you want to live your best life? Do you want to have the best marriage? You are going to have to die to who you have been in order to grow into the woman God wants you to be. But the most wonderful news is that He will hold your hand and carry you every step of the way.

Sister, look to the Lord today. He is the only "soulmate" you will ever need! Ask Him to show you the ways He wants you to grow in your walk with Him and follow Him in your marriage. Pray that God would replace your fleshly heart with His pure heart of love, compassion, and forgiveness for your husband. Pray that God would show you how to love your husband in the way Christ loves you. I promise, when you walk in this way, there is so much joy and peace ahead!! He has beautiful plans for you and your marriage!

Love in Christ,
Tara Davis and the Help Club for Moms Team

> *Marriage is one of the most humbling, sanctifying journeys you will ever be a part of. It forces us to wrestle with our selfishness and pride. But it also gives us a platform to display love and commitment.*
> ~ Francis Chan, "You and Me Forever: Marriage in Light of Eternity"

Mom Tips

By: Leslie Leonard

"Let your roots grow down into him, and let your lives be built on him.
Then your faith will grow strong in the truth you were taught,
and you will overflow with thankfulness." ~ Colossians 2:7 (NLT)

The Wise Woman Builds Her Spirit

- Before getting out of bed in the morning, commit your day to God. Acknowledge God's sovereignty over the day and ask God to help you accept His plan for you.

- For a simple and cheap luxury, use this simple recipe: Mix brown sugar and olive oil together to use as a hand, foot, or lip scrub.

The Wise Woman Loves Her Husband

- If your husband wears a suit or collared shirts to work, spend some time ironing and folding his clothes. Write a sweet note saying "Ironed with Love," and fold it or hang it with the garment where he will find it when getting dressed.

- Let your husband sleep in or take a nap, guilt-free! Consider taking the kids out of the house while he rests to give him peace and quiet.

The Wise Woman Loves Her Children

- Commit to only using positive and uplifting words when speaking to your children for at least two days this week. Let your children see you always ready with a kind word and a helpful hand.

- Let your children plan the dinner menu one night this week. After the menu is set, get them involved in preparing the meal that night. Small hands can help wash vegetables, set the table, etc.

The Wise Woman Cares For Her Home

- Stop to consider what in your routine is not working for your family, and find a new solution. Don't be afraid to cut something out of your schedule in order to give your family more time together.

- Stick to your family budget this week. Don't buy anything that is not budgeted for in your plan. If you do not have a family budget, sit down and create one with your spouse.

Love Your Husband

~ CHALLENGE ~

Do you find your marriage growing stale and in need of revival?
Perhaps you desire more intentionality as a wife?
Sister, I can tell you that this challenge will change things for you,
just as it has for me. Commit with me to hiding these Scriptures and
new habits in your heart this week. Just growing more purposeful
in these small ways will awaken beauty in your marriage!

Challenge

DAY 1

"A soft answer turns away wrath, but a harsh word stirs up anger. The tongue of the wise uses knowledge rightly, but the mouth of fools pours forth foolishness."

~ Proverbs 15:1-2 (NKJV)

Do you find yourself speaking harshly to your husband?
It is so easy to do, but our words have the power to either destroy
or to create new life in the heart of our husbands. Choose life!
When you speak words of life, you will be filled with peace as well.

Faith-Filled Idea:

If you feel like making a negative comment to your husband today,
close your lips and instead open your heart to the Lord in prayer.
It is better to say nothing than to say something damaging or regretful.

Speak only kind words today and for the remainder of the week.
Choose one thing you can thank your husband for or compliment him on each day.
This new habit will become easier and easier as you practice.

Prayer:

*Lord, give me words that bring life to my husband.
Fill my heart with self-control, that I would be able to honor You
in all I say and do in my marriage.*

Journal

Challenge

_____
_____
_____
_____
_____
_____
_____
_____
_____
_____
_____
_____
_____
_____
_____
_____
_____
_____
_____
_____
_____
_____
_____
_____
_____
_____
_____

Love Your Husband

~ CHALLENGE ~

DAY 2

"Finally, brothers and sisters, whatever is true, whatever is noble, whatever is right,
whatever is pure, whatever is lovely, whatever is admirable—
if anything is excellent or praiseworthy—think about such things."

~ Philippians 4:8

Do you struggle with negative thoughts toward your husband?
Do you ever feel hopeless in your marriage? This is not God's intention for you as a wife!
He wants you to think pure, admirable, true thoughts.
As you think about your marriage, so it becomes!
Begin today by becoming a wife who finds the best in her husband and who makes those
positive qualities the focus of her thoughts and the highlights of her marriage!

Faith-Filled Idea:

Make a list of attributes you appreciate about your husband.
Even if the list is short for now, I promise it will grow!

Every time you think something negative about your husband or marriage, immediately
replace that negative thought by thinking on the things you admire about your man.
It is amazing how, over time, this practice will change your perception of
your husband and your marriage! It feels good to notice the good!

Prayer:

Lord, help me love my husband more today than ever before.
Remind me of the qualities I love about Him,
and help my thoughts remain honoring to You!

journal

Challenge

Love Your Husband

~ CHALLENGE ~

DAY 3

"Dear children, let us not love with words or speech but with actions and in truth."
~ 1 John 3:18

Let your actions communicate your love and the love of Christ to your husband today!
Words of love are wonderful, but actions need to line up
with words for your statement of love to have value.
Do you ever find yourself growing lax in the area of showing your husband love?
Today is the day to love your man well in word and in deed!

Faith-Filled Idea:

What is one thing you can do for your husband that speaks volumes of your love?
Perhaps it is getting up early to make his coffee or pack his lunch,
cleaning an area of the house that bothers him, or initiating intimacy.

Prayer:

Lord, please give me insight into my husband's heart.
Help me to know the areas which will best communicate love to him today.
Show me how to shower him with the love of Christ!

Challenge

journal

Challenge

10 Scriptures to pray for your Husband

1. *Pray that your husband would know the depth of God's love for him.*
   Ephesians 3:18: "That you may have power, together with all the Lord's holy people, to grasp how wide and long and high and deep is the love of Christ."

2. *Pray that your husband lives in accordance with God's plan for his life.*
   Ephesians 4:1-2: "I, therefore, the prisoner of the Lord, beseech you to walk worthy of the calling with which you were called, with all lowliness and gentleness, with longsuffering, bearing with one another in love."

3. *Pray that the Lord would bless your husband's work.*
   Proverbs 22:29: "Do you see a man who excels in his work? He will stand before kings; He will not stand before unknown men."

4. *Pray that God would make him a man of integrity.*
   Proverbs 11:3: "The integrity of the upright will guide them, but the perversity of the unfaithful will destroy them."

5. *Pray that God would strengthen him to resist temptation.*
   1 Corinthians 10:13: "No temptation has overtaken you except such as is common to man; but God is faithful, who will not allow you to be tempted beyond what you are able, but with the temptation will also make the way of escape, that you may be able to bear it."

6. *Pray that your husband would desire wisdom and seek it diligently.*
   James 1:5: "If any of you lacks wisdom, let him ask of God, who gives to all liberally and without reproach, and it will be given to him."

7. *Pray that your husband would trust in the Lord for his strength.*
   Psalm 28:7: "The Lord is my strength and my shield; my heart trusted in Him, and I am helped; therefore my heart greatly rejoices, and with my song I will praise Him."

8. *Pray that your husband will surround himself with godly friends and wise mentors.*
   Proverbs 13:20: "He who walks with wise men will be wise, but the companion of fools will be destroyed."

9. *That he would be full of patience and peace.*
   Romans 14:19: "Therefore let us pursue the things which make for peace and the things by which one may edify another."

10. *Pray for your husband to love you and your children with the love of Jesus.*
    John 13:34: "A new command I give you: Love one another. As I have loved you, so you must love one another."

Love Your Husband

CHALLENGE

~ Week Thirteen ~

Dearest Mama,

I recently read the quote by Denis Avery, a prisoner of war survivor who was held in a Nazi work camp next to Auschwitz during World War II. He said, "The mind is a powerful thing, it can take you through walls." What an incredible testimony to the power of our thoughts!

Prison camps aren't the only things that have walls. Our relationships, particularly our marriages, can have huge walls that feel as if they could never be broken down. And just like Avery's quote, our thoughts about our husbands and the quality of our marriages can build up or break down those walls.

The Bible says in Proverbs 4:23, "Above all else, guard your heart, for it is the wellspring of life."

God wants us to guard our hearts, and how we do this is by watching what we think about. If you were to be brutally honest, what are the day-in and day-out thoughts you allow yourself to think about your man? Do you see your marriage in a positive light, even if it's not perfect, or do you constantly nitpick about the things that have gone wrong and are disappointing?

Friend, our thoughts matter more than we know. How about trying to realign your thoughts this week according to the hope that is found in God's Word? Instead of thinking defeating thoughts, begin to ask God to help you to believe that He is with you and is working to make your marriage better all the time.

Begin to speak like God does in Romans 4:17 (ESV) where He, "...gives life to the dead and calls into existence the things that do not exist." Today, try to speak words of life and hope over your marriage. Say things like, "God is with us and has great plans for our marriage," "I am so glad I married my man," or "My husband loves me."

What's the worst thing that could happen? God may surprise you and bring the miracle you have been praying for as you trust in Him.

I am praying for you today.

Love,
Deb Weakly and the Help Club For Moms Team

" *You cannot have a positive life and a negative mind.* "
~ *Joyce Meyer*

Mom Tips

By: Leslie Leonard

"Let your roots grow down into him, and let your lives be built on him. Then your faith will grow strong in the truth you were taught, and you will overflow with thankfulness." ~ Colossians 2:7 (NLT)

The Wise Woman Builds Her Spirit

- Spend extra time this week praying for a specific trial or issue in your family. Pray for the Holy Spirit to intervene with guidance.

- Do a 24-hour social media "fast" this week. Put away your smartphone and unplug from all the distractions. Use the time to pray, meditate, or spend time with your family. Consider making a commitment to spend less time on your phone in the future.

The Wise Woman Loves Her Husband

- Eat dinner together as a family at least 3 times this week. Sit down and enjoy your family. Have each person share their "highs and lows" from the day.

- Do something for your husband this week in his love language to show him that you love him. If you want to know what your husband's (and your) love language is, complete the assessment online at https://www.5lovelanguages.com/.

The Wise Woman Loves Her Children

- Serve your community. On a nice day, grab a trash bag and some gloves. Take your kids to clean up trash around your neighborhood or park.

- Place a note in your kids' lunch box telling them how much you love them and how special they are. If you homeschool, place a note under their lunch plate. Pinterest has many cute, free printables to keep this entertaining and special.

The Wise Woman Cares For Her Home

- Make an extra batch of cookies or zucchini bread to cheer up a friend who has had a bad day or to share with a neighbor or mom friend who might need a visit from a friendly face. You never know when you might be the only person someone has talked to that day.

- Do you have unworn clothes taking up room in your closets? Clothes that you look at and say, "I'll wear that someday" or "In 10 pounds that will fit." Grab a box or bag and get those clothes out of your home. Reduce your clutter and only keep the items in your closet that you use and wear. It will reduce the stress and anxiety you feel when getting ready in the morning, and it will bless someone else who will wear it now.

Love Your Husband

~ CHALLENGE ~

DAY 4

"Bear with each other and forgive one another if any of you has a grievance against someone.
Forgive as the Lord forgave you."

~ Colossians 3:13

Has your husband wronged you?
Regardless of the offense, carrying unforgiveness in your heart is a burden the Lord
does not want you to bear. Cast your cares on the Lord today. He loves you so much.
Choose to forgive your husband for all things, large and small,
and you will reap the reward of peace in your life!

Faith-Filled Idea:

Take just a moment to ponder how greatly our blameless Lord has forgiven you.
How much more should we, fellow sinners, forgive our husbands?
Pray and ask the Lord to help you forgive. With Him, all things are possible!

If it helps you to release the burden of unforgiveness you bear,
write your burden on a slip of paper, light it on fire, and drop it into a glass jar.

Observe the ashes left behind and be encouraged;
Jesus makes beautiful things from the ashes in our lives!
Whenever you feel like picking up that burden again,
continue to lay it at the foot of the cross.
It is not yours to carry, sister.

Prayer:

Lord, please heal my heart. Show me how to forgive my husband.
I give you my burdens now and do not want to pick them up again.
Please bring healing into our marriage.

journal

Challenge

_____
_____
_____
_____
_____
_____
_____
_____
_____
_____
_____
_____
_____
_____
_____
_____
_____
_____
_____
_____
_____
_____
_____
_____

Love Your Husband

~ CHALLENGE ~

DAY 5

"Do nothing from selfishness or empty conceit,
but with humility of mind regard one another as more important than yourselves;
do not merely look out for your own personal interests, but also for the interests of others."

~ Philippians 2:3-4 (NASB)

What are your husband's deepest needs?
Often our husband's "love language" is different than ours.
Sometimes we need to lay ourselves and our own desires down to love our husband well.
What is God asking you to lay down in your marriage?
Ponder for a moment what would make your husband's life easier and bring peace to his heart.

Faith-Filled Idea:

It's a counter-cultural concept in our society to consider others before ourselves.
But the message of Christ is to die to ourselves so that we will be able to live for Him.
In doing so, we are able to love others through His power.
Consider your husband's needs and how you can unselfishly serve him through the love of Christ.
Choose a particular need to meet today.

Prayer:

Lord, please show me how to surrender myself to You and to love my husband selflessly.
Bring peace to my heart in the knowledge that I can consider his needs first because
YOU are the one who meets all my needs according to YOUR glorious riches!!

Journal

Love Your Husband
CHALLENGE ~

DAY 6

*"Do not be anxious about anything, but in every situation,
by prayer and petition, with thanksgiving, present your requests to God"*

~ Philippians 4:6

It is easy to stress about life, marriage, and parenting.
But that is not God's best for us! God wants us to bring our concerns to him.
Praising God for your husband and praying for his needs and his heart is
guaranteed to be one of your most rewarding works as his wife.
There is so much peace that comes from praying for your husband!

Faith-Filled Idea:

Take your husband to the Lord in prayer!
Ask your husband how you can pray for him or simply pray for needs you are aware of.
Pray for his heart, that he will know the deep love of God.
Pray that the Holy Spirit will strengthen him to resist temptation.
Pray that He will love the Lord and his family more than ever before.
Pray the Lord's blessing over him. Pray for every little area of his life.
The task of praying for your husband will be one that will last a lifetime,
but is also one of the greatest gifts you can give him!

Prayer:

*Lord, please show me how to pray for my husband.
Help me not to complain about him to you, but to truly lift him up to you in love.
Change my heart where it needs to be changed and give me the energy
to really pray for the man you have given me.*

journal

_____

_____

_____

_____

_____

_____

_____

_____

_____

_____

_____

_____

_____

_____

_____

_____

_____

_____

_____

_____

_____

_____

_____

_____

Challenge

Food for the Soul

Our husbands can easily be put on the back burner of our busy lives in this season of rearing young children. Driving older children around from activity to activity, helping with homework, baking for class parties, and trying to make meaningful memories for our kids and families is certainly time consuming. We don't want our men to feel like they aren't a priority in our busy lives.

I recently learned that, as women, we are constantly being complimented and given positive feedback from our female family members, friends, and coworkers. It's natural for us to tell each other when we think another looks cute or that the food they cooked is amazing. Men, however, do not receive this constant flow of positive or complimentary feedback, especially in their work environment where they spend the majority of their waking hours. It's just not how men relate to one another naturally. This means we *need* to make sure that our guy knows that he means the world to us and that we truly appreciate all he does, big and small.

I challenge you, ladies, to set aside a night in the next couple of weeks to surprise your man with an extra special dinner. Make it as homemade as you can. Plan some alone time for you and your hubby, or include the whole family. When your husband walks in the door, have everyone waiting to greet him all dressed up, with candles lit, and your special meal ready. During the meal, take the time to tell your man all the things you appreciate about him and what he means to your family.

To make this dinner extra special, make sure you include dessert! What guy doesn't love to finish a meal off with a special sweet treat? I have just the dessert for you: Homemade Tiramisu. My husband loves when I make this because he knows I am going out of my way to make it for him.

This recipe is a labor of love, but I do have a few little shortcuts to make it easier. It is great fresh, but actually gets better 24-48 hours after you prepare it; so, if time permits, make it a day or two before your special dinner. Constructing it ahead of time also allows extra time the night you cook your special dinner. Your dessert will already be taken care of! I hope you give it a try and that it blesses your man.

TIRAMISU By: Brandi Carson

Ingredients for Lady Fingers:

4 eggs, separated   ⅞ cup all-purpose flour
⅔ cup white sugar   ½ teaspoon baking powder

Directions:

1. Preheat oven to 400 degrees.

2. Line two 17 x 12" baking sheets with parchment paper. On the back side of the parchment paper, use a pencil to draw rows width-wise to create a template to pipe out uniform ladyfingers. When marking the parchment, be sure to leave at least a 1-inch space between the template rows to keep the ladyfingers from connecting on the top and bottom during baking. The size and shape of the dish that is being used to make the Tiramisu will determine how long the ladyfingers should be, but I usually make them 3 to 4 inches long.

Lady Finger Directions: (Continued)

3. Prep a pastry bag or heavy-duty gallon plastic bag with a ½" round frosting tip.

4. In a medium bowl, beat egg whites on high until soft peaks form.

5. Slowly add 2 tablespoons of sugar and continue beating until the egg whites are stiff and glossy.

6. In a separate medium bowl, beat egg yolks and remaining sugar together until very pale in color.

7. In another bowl, sift together flour and baking powder.

8. Fold together half of the egg whites into the egg yolk mixture. Next, fold in the flour mixture until well combined, then fold in the remaining egg white mixture until it is also well combined.

9. Gently scoop out mixture and place into piping bag.

10. Pipe out groups of three ladyfingers onto parchment template, leaving at least 1-inch of space between each grouping. The batter will spread out quite a bit, so when piping each group of ladyfingers, they should not touch before baking. When piping the group of three, leave about ½" of space between each individual ladyfinger. This will allow them to spread out some but still connect during baking. Baking groups of three ladyfingers allows for quicker assembly of the Tiramisu later. If you want individual ladyfingers, keep them at least 1 inch apart to keep them from baking together.

11. Bake for 7-10 minutes. Individual ladyfingers will bake more quickly than grouped ones. You want to pull them out of the oven at the first sign of browning or slightly before. Ladyfingers are very blonde sugar cookies. Let cool completely before assembly.

Ingredients for Tiramisu:

6 egg yolks

¾ cup white sugar

1 ¼ cup heavy cream

½ teaspoon vanilla

16 ounces mascarpone cheese

½ cup strong brewed coffee or coffee concentrate, room temperature

2 (3 ounce) packages of ladyfingers, or one recipe of homemade ladyfingers above

1 tablespoon unsweetened cocoa powder

Food for the Soul

Directions for Tiramisu:

1. In a medium saucepan, whisk together egg yolks and sugar until well blended. Whisk in milk and cook over medium heat, whisking constantly until mixture boils. Boil gently for 1 minute, remove from heat, and allow to cool slightly. Transfer custard to a bowl, then whisk in mascarpone cheese until creamy and completely incorporated.

2. Once mascarpone is mixed in, cover tightly, and chill for 1 hour in the refrigerator.

3. While the custard is cooling in a medium bowl, beat cream with vanilla until stiff peaks form. Keep refrigerated until custard is completely cooled and set up.

4. Once the custard is completely cold, gently fold whipped cream mixture into custard.

5. Pour strong coffee into a medium, flat, shallow dish; an 8 x 8 baking dish works great.

6. Have your serving dish for the Tiramisu ready. You can use a 7 x 11" baking dish or a trifle bowl if you want to get fancy. First, you will quickly dip ladyfingers in coffee and flip. Do not let them soak too long or the ladyfingers get soggy and become difficult to handle.

7. Line the bottom of the dish with soaked ladyfingers. If you are using a trifle bowl, you will now line the outside of the trifle dish with unsoaked ladyfingers standing up facing outwards. This part can be a little tricky to keep them from falling over before the bowl is filled, so wedge them all the way to the bottom between the layer of soaked flat-laying ladyfingers and the glass.

8. You are now ready to add the filling layers. If you are using a flat 7 x 11" dish, you will spread half of the filling over the soaked ladyfingers. If using a trifle bowl, you may only need ⅓ to ¼ of the filling, depending on the size of your trifle bowl. When the filling is evenly spread over ladyfingers, repeat.

9. Once all layers are done, dust the top generously with cocoa. Cover and refrigerate overnight. For best results, make at least 24 hours ahead to allow all the flavors to meld together.

Help Club for Moms

Help Club For Moms is a community of moms who encourage one another to know the love of Jesus Christ. Our ministry cultivates mom-to-mom relationships through social media platforms and programs for small groups and churches. We believe that prayer changes everything and that God is big enough to help us raise our children...even in today's culture. We focus on digging into God's Word, praying together, and seeking to become the women, wives, and mothers God created us to be.

Would you like to be a part of the movement?

Here's how you can get involved in the Help Club for Moms:

- Purchase our books on Amazon. We use 100% of the proceeds to fund our all-volunteer ministry. The titles are: *The Help Club for Moms* (Harvest House Publishers), *The Help Club for Mom Companion Guide*, *The Wise Woman Believes*, *The Wise Woman Loves*, *The Wise Woman Stays*, *The Wise Woman Abides*, *The Wise Woman Grows*, *The Wise Woman Enjoys*, *Holidays with the Help Club*, and *The 40-Day Joy Challenge for Moms*.

- Pray for the ministry and the moms in our Help Club Community worldwide—for them to know the love of Jesus and create a Christ-like atmosphere in their homes.

- Start a Help Club for Moms group at your local church or home. We can help you! (See pages 205-212).

- We are always on the lookout for Titus 2 women who can help mentor our moms through social media and prayer.

- If you are an author, blogger, graphics artist, or social media guru, we need you and your talents at the Help Club!

- We are a 501(c)(3) an all-volunteer ministry! Please go to HelpClubForMoms.com to partner with us to get God's Word into the hands of moms worldwide!

You can find out more about Help Club for Moms at HelpClubForMoms.com and on Facebook and Instagram @HelpClubForMoms.

Donate Here:

....

Please help us receive funding at no cost to you!

Did you know that Help Club for Moms is now listed as a non-profit 501(c)(3) on Amazon Smile? Yes, we are! And you can help us reach moms around the world by selecting Help Club for Moms as your designated ministry under your Amazon account. Then, for every eligible purchase, Help Club for Moms receives .05% of your purchase price!

It's easy to join! Simply go to smile.amazon.com and log in to your Amazon account. Search the list of charities and select Help Club for Moms. Then shop! You must log in through smile.amazon.com each time for your purchase to be counted as a donation, or click smile before ordering under your regular Amazon account login.

Church Resource
Section

Help Club
for
Moms

Dear Mom,

We are so very honored that you are journeying through this Bible study with us. What a gift you are to our ministry!

We wanted to make sure you knew that, built right into this book, is everything you need to start a "Help Club for Moms" group of your own! You can do it through your church or even as a small group in your home. Lives are changed when we read God's Word together and focus on becoming intentional moms and wives in community together! Doing a Help Club for Moms Bible Study is a chance for you and your friends to dive deeper into learning about God's design for motherhood. Plus, everything is more fun with friends!

It is so easy to lead a Help Club for Moms group. Each mom commits to following along in the Bible study. Then you meet at your home or church just twice per month to go over what you are learning and pray for one another. We even have a special place on our website called "Leaders Resources" where you can find helpful videos and materials for your group.

Doing life together as moms in a Christ-centered community draws us closer to Jesus and to each other while building friendships and connections that are sure to last a lifetime. What a great way to walk as moms, together, arm-in-arm, and with our eyes on Jesus all the way until we get to heaven!

If you are interested in starting a Help Club for Moms group, either in your church or home, please email us at admin@helpclubformoms.com. We would love to walk alongside you, give you helpful resources, and PRAY for you.

Blessings to you, mama!

Sincerely,
The Help Club for Moms Team

FAQ:
About Help Club For Moms

WHAT IS THE HELP CLUB FOR MOMS?

• Help Club for Moms is a community of moms encouraging moms to know the love of Christ. We value authentic, transparent relationships. Together, we study God's Word, pray, fellowship twice a month, and share practical "Mom Tips." All this to become the women, wives, and mothers God created us to be, and with the help of the Holy Spirit, bring up our children to do the same!

WHY CHOOSE HELP CLUB?

• Help Club For Moms offers a Christ-centered program focused on strengthening the church by strengthening moms, through teaching God's design for families and biblically based parenting.

• There is no fee for the program; the only cost is for the books which may be purchased on Amazon.

• The program is for moms of all ages. We love learning from each other in every stage of life!

• There are three simple, but deep, biblical studies per week, which teach and encourage moms, yet are still easy to accomplish. A must for today's busy mom!

• Help Club For Moms "Mom Tips" set us apart from other mom groups because every week, we offer eight practical, new ideas to strengthen and train women in their role as a wife, mother, and woman of God.

• Each mom in Help Club For Moms is partnered with another mom for prayer. Every week, these two moms pray for 10-15 minutes with one another over the phone, deepening their connection with God and each other. Prayer changes everything!

• Help Club For Moms brings godly community, support, fellowship, and friendship to families through the relationships formed between moms.

• HCFM's has three years of Christ-centered curriculum.

• HCFM has a strong presence on social media, which helps moms go deeper in the studies with other moms around the world.

WHAT ARE THE CORE VALUES OF HELP CLUB FOR MOMS?

• HCFM values authentic and transparent community between moms, deep growth in relationship with God, intentional Bible study, faithful prayer relationships between moms, and practical day-to-day ideas and tips for moms.

WHAT IS REQUIRED OF THE CHURCH?

• HCFM's partner churches should plan to help in two ways:

    1. Offer a meeting space for two hours/twice monthly

    2. Help with childcare for two hours/twice monthly

Hosting a HCFM's Meeting

WHAT DOES A TYPICAL HELP CLUB FOR MOMS MEETING LOOK LIKE?

Hosting a Help Club meeting is easy and fun and is a great way to build community with the moms in your church or neighborhood. Below is a sample morning meeting schedule. (You could also host a "Help Club Mom's Night Out Potluck Dinner" instead of a daytime meeting for working moms or moms who want some time away while dad has the children.)

SCHEDULE

9:30 - 9:40 **Welcome, pray, and on time drawing with an inexpensive prize**

9:40 - 10:00 **Simple worship and announcements** (HCFM Spotify playlist website link on pg. 212)

10:00 - 10:30 **Moms meet in groups to discuss current HCFM Bible study**
- Large groups: Moms sit around tables in small groups of 3-6 moms with a leader and possible co-leader to discuss content from the last two week's topic.
- Small groups or home study group: Moms sit in a circle as one big group to discuss content from the last two week's topic.

10:30 - 10:35 **Book Review** (HCFM suggested book review provided if desired)

10:35 - 10:50 **Mom Tips in Action** (Invite one of your leaders/ helpers to spotlight a Mom Tip from this week's study and how she used it) Then, invite other moms from the group to share how they used a moms tip from the list or how they are planning to use one in the future. This is an important time for our moms to learn from each other.

10:50 - 11:15 **Devotion time**
There are two ways to facilitate a HCFM's devotion portion of the group: one led by a seasoned mom or one led by a young, peer aged mom.
- Both groups lead a discussion about the topic from the last two weeks of study by discussing the Scriptures read, Questions to Ponder, or Faith-Filled Ideas. The leader could also share her personal experience as a fellow mom journeying on the road of motherhood. The leader may also choose to watch the small group teaching video (with selected Help Club books), which are available at no charge on the Help Club for Moms website under the "Leader Resources" section. You may also choose to watch one of the Mentoring Monday videos available each week. These are found on the Help Club for Moms Facebook page, the Help Club for Moms YouTube channel, and our podcast.

11:15 - 11:25 **Moms pray with prayer partners**

11:25 **Pray and dismiss moms to pick up children**

Note: All HCFM leaders have access to a special area on our website at helpclubformoms.com just for leaders called "Leader Resources." There we offer videos to help you get your Help Club started, videos to train your small group leaders, and also teaching session videos and lesson plans for many of our books. **Questions? Email us at admin@helpclubformoms.com.**

Book Recommendations

BOOKS FOR MOMS (NON-FICTION):

Parenting the Wholehearted Child
  by Jeannie Cunnion

You and Me Forever by Francis and Lisa Chan
  (marriage)

The Ragamuffin Gospel by Brennan Manning

Love and Respect by Dr. Emmerson Eggerichs

Love and Respect in the Family
  by Dr. Emmerson Eggerichs

Mother and Son by Dr. Emmerson Eggerichs

The Circle Maker by Mark Batterson

The Power of a Praying Wife
  by Stormie O' Martian

The Power of a Praying Parent
  by Stormie O' Martian

The Read-Aloud Family by Sarah Mackenzie

Boy Mom by Monica Swanson

BOOKS FOR MOMS (FICTION):

Mark of the Lion trilogy by Francine Rivers

Redeeming Love by Francine Rivers

Sarah's Key by Tatiana de Rosnay

The Help by Kathryn Stockett

BOOKS FOR KIDS:

Discipleship books:

The Picture Bible published by David C. Cook

The Jesus Storybook Bible by Sally Lloyd-Jones

Missionary Stories with the Millers
  by Mildred A. Martin

The Christian Heroes: Then & Now series

The Action Bible by Sergio Cariello

BibleForce: The First Heroes Bible

The Case for Christ for Kids series

Upper Elementary/Early Middle School (grades 4-7):

The Wingfeather Saga by Andrew Peterson

The Green Ember series by E.D. Smith

The Penderwicks series by Jeanne Birdsall

Lower Elementary (grades 2-3):

The Imagination Station by Marianne Hering

Greetings from Somewhere by Harper Paris

Dear Molly, Dear Olive by Megan Atwood

Early Readers (grades K-1):

Owl Diaries by Rebecca Elliot

I Can Read! Princess Parables by Jeanna Young

Jotham's Journey series

Little House on the Prairie by Laura Ingalls Wilder

The BFG by Roald Dahl

The Lion, The Witch, and the Wardrobe
  by C.S. Lewis

Anne of Green Gables by Lucy Maud Montgomery

HOMESCHOOLING:

Teaching From Rest by Sarah Mackenzie

Educating the WholeHearted Child
  by Clay Clarkson with Sally Clarkson

Seasons of a Mother's Heart by Sally Clarkson

Podcasts

PODCASTS FOR MOMS:

Help Club for Moms

Don't Mom Alone

Coffee & Crumbs

Java with Juli

Cultivating the Lovely

Parenting Great Kids with Dr. Meg Meeker

Focus on the Family

The Messenger Podcast

Conversations with John and Lisa Bevere

I am Adamant Podcast by Lisa Bevere

Read Aloud Revival

Happy Hour with Jamie Ivey

PODCASTS FOR KIDS:

Stories Podcast

Storynory

Brains On! Science Podcast for Kids

Adventures in Odyssey

ONLINE SERMONS:

ChurchoftheHighlands.org

Theaterchurch.org

Newlifechurch.org

Worship Music

SPOTIFY HELP CLUB FOR MOMS STATION:

https://spoti.fi/2lVBMbw

Plan Sheets

Daily Plan

Date: _____

M T W T F S S

Weekly Memory Verse:

"

"

3 Things I am Grateful for Today:

1.

2.

3.

Notes:

6 Most Important List:

1.

2.

3.

4.

5.

6.

Meal Planning:

Breakfast:

Lunch:

Dinner:

Cleaning:

O 15-min. area _____

O 5'o clock pick-up

Weekly Plan

	Sunday	Monday	Tuesday	Wednesday	Thursday	Friday	Saturday
6:00							
7:00							
8:00							
9:00							
10:00							
11:00							
12:00							
1:00							
2:00							
3:00							
4:00							
5:00							
6:00							
7:00							
8:00							
9:00							
10:00							

Daily Plan

Date: _____

M T W T F S S

Weekly Memory Verse:

"

"

3 Things I am Grateful for Today:

1.

2.

3.

Notes:

6 Most Important List:

1.

2.

3.

4.

5.

6.

Meal Planning:

Breakfast:

Lunch:

Dinner:

Cleaning:

O 15-min. area _____

O 5'o clock pick-up

Weekly Plan

	Sunday	Monday	Tuesday	Wednesday	Thursday	Friday	Saturday
6:00							
7:00							
8:00							
9:00							
10:00							
11:00							
12:00							
1:00							
2:00							
3:00							
4:00							
5:00							
6:00							
7:00							
8:00							
9:00							
10:00							